Tom Law has lived in East Gippsland, Victoria, Australia for a period of nigh on forty years. Originally from England (but born in Glasgow), he was educated at Melbourne High School and later at Monash University. He describes his academic progress as chequered. "The problem with education is that it can get in the way of living..." But Tom never lets the dust settle under his feet and seriously views learning as his life-blood along with exploration of everything. As a teacher of IT, Mathematics and Science, he has worked in many different countries, Indonesia and China in particular.

Building his life and home 'among the gum trees' he developed a deep affinity and love for the natural environment of this unique part of Australia. "Very few places experience the convergence of bird life from such a wide range of habitats... forest, high plains and coastal dwellers all breeze in and out of this area, depending on the season and prevailing weather. Migratory types such as swallows visit from as far away as China. When I first came here as a young man I could distinguish between a wattle tree and a eucalyptus but that is where it ended. Now I can view a Blackwood and differentiate it from a variety of these trees."

Tom built his first house from natural materials at hand... stone, timber, slate and whatever could be recycled from earlier building materials left over from the gold era of the mid-nineteenth century. "So many cultures have made an impact on this area in a brief frenetic period of gold mining. They came from China, Europe and North America in search of their fortunes. Some stayed, some died penniless and others returned home after some success. What now takes less than a two hour drive to a large regional town took three days at least by wagon and horse. The local cemetery tells tales of woe and grief from a bygone age of hardship and struggle difficult to comprehend in modern times."

Tom has two adult sons from his first marriage plus a daughter and son from his second marriage to an Indonesian lady.

guns off cops…

guns off everyone!

☆ LONGERSHIP ☆

☆ LIBERTY ☆

Tom Law

This book is for the peoples of the world

... that they may find everlasting peace

and put an end to tyranny

Also for my friends:

Lilly A. and in memory of Ronald M.

ISBN   9780994315779

Published in Australia by:
Longership Publishing Australia
Swifts Creek Victoria 3896 AUSTRALIA
ABN 73446736413
email: longership@email.com

First published in Australia 2016
Copyright © Tom Law
Cover design Tom Law

The right of Tom Law to be identified as the Author of the Work has been asserted in accordance with   the Copyright, Designs and Patents Act 1988.

Law, Tom
Guns Off Cops Guns Off Everyone
ISBN: 9780994315779
pp 252

Contents

Introduction

At first you might think that this book is primarily about armed police. I must inform you at the outset that whilst there is reference to armed police and consequential police shootings, the focus is on guns in general, how they are obtained and the whole money machine of conflict and misery around the world due to the entrepreneurial element of gun sales. Further, I peruse and pursue the big business of international arms dealings, legal and illegal with the apparent consequences of human misery on an unprecedented scale in the world we live in at the early part of the twenty first century.

Also, what this book is not: it is not an attack on the police which the author sees as generally a dedicated group of professionals trying their level best to uphold the laws of the country. A police force is both necessary and essential in any society, and always will be. They more often than not deserve praise for the work they do.

I recently watched the movie 'Runaway Jury' (2003), based on the novel by John Grisham (1996) where a gun manufacturer was held complicit in a mass shooting due to the fact that they irresponsibly allowed both excessive and illegal gun sales. They were fined (in the movie) a little over 100 million dollars. I am uncertain as to whether in real life any such successful legal action has ever taken place and it disturbs me that it was written over twenty years ago! I agree wholeheartedly with the thrust that *"gun manufacturers should be held complicit with regard to mass murder by guns"*

Murder, wars and mayhem seem to be constantly in the news. It is easy to point the finger at religion as a cause of this suffering. Others point to race and racial hatred. And others still to the squabbles between

9

sovereign states over borders and land acquisition (including the sea bed and remote islands no more than a patch of sand or a piece of rock inhabited by sea birds with no understanding of what the fuss is all about!) As for myself, I look to both the fomenters of conflict and those companies and industries in arms and chemicals that see war as a lucrative business opportunity. These owners of warehouses and production lines are the true enemies of humanity in today's world and need to be punished in the world's courts and their activities curbed (along with illegal drug manufacturers) if we are ever to move forward to a more peaceful and safer world.

My stomach turns when I see armed police or quasi-military brigades on our streets with fully automatic weapons whilst politicians continue to spout like a cracked recording: "we are just keeping you all safe!"

My irritation rises just seeing any police on our streets carrying a side-arm when chances are it will never be used (I am referring to Australia at this time).

I am fearful to walk even in the CBD of New York City for a potential 'hard rain' of lead coming my way. I am disgusted at the statistics from our close ally regarding shooting deaths each year and especially those deaths and murders perpetrated by a few US law enforcers.

Those of my fellow countrymen that continue to argue that it is "not the guns that kill or maim people, but the persons holding the gun" do not impress with such a simple argument (as well as stating the obvious!)

One is one thousand times more likely to be shot by a policeman or some nutter with a gun than by a so called political or religious terrorist. Yet, from the few incidences of terrorism in Western countries, a large segment of society is now under suspicion and, in many quarters hated, to a level not seen since fascism overtook Europe in the 1930's. In fact statistics show that you are more likely to be murdered by someone you know i.e a relative or a neighbour than by a complete stranger.

Political extremist groups now flourish in my country as well as in the US and many European countries purportedly labelled civilised. These groups feed on fear mongering, simplicity of

Pauline Hanson of One Nation

rhetoric and a thirst for blood and violence. In Australia the basis of this fear is non-existent. I can only guess at a disturbing high number of low intelligent people along with thugs and the bland and ignorant members of our society! We saw it with the Jews in the 1930's and now we are seeing similar beginnings and tendencies with Muslims. In rural Australia recently a heavy accented lady of French extraction was heard to say "why do they want mosques? Why can they not eat ham sandwiches like us normal Ozzies. Why don't they accept our ways?" Hopefully someone will take Ms Hanson to court for spreading racial and religious hatred!

I had no energy to confront the mind of a village peasant but later reflected: Jews don't eat pork. Many young Australians these days are vegetarians or vegans. Few people claiming loosely to be Christians refrain from eating meat on a Friday. Our nation has drifted more towards greed and hedonism with the loss of survivalist values in recent decades, so why such an outpouring on one group making up our rich multicultural society? The vast majority of citizens are law abiding and contribute to our nation so why single out a particular group because they worship God differently and don't eat piggy wiggy?

I would really like to see the words Church, Temple, Synagogue, Mosque disappear from our everyday language to be replaced simply by "Place of Worship" thus attempting to remove in a small way any specific reference to a particular "one God religion"… just a thought!

The other thrust of this tome is about the manufacturers and dealers in arms. The sad truth is that there is a lot of money to be made out of selling arms and armaments from the simplest rifle or pistol to fighter jets, ballistic missiles, ships, submarines and bombs of various strengths and descriptions. It is a wicked web and the absolute worst part of capitalism where vast sums of money are made from tiny wars between factions. It is the lowest common denominator of free enterprise. But you know, it starts with the US constitution in that country and the powerful political clout of the National Rifle Association that maintains the stance that every citizen has the right to be a cowboy and carry a six gun or worse! Not only does it bring horrific statistics of gun deaths but perpetuates a psyche that cannot easily be shaken off where weaponry and shooting are a natural and expected way of life. Putting human tragedy aside, can the environment along with its fauna sustain such attitudes and onslaught long into the future? My country has an enormous land mass and small population so it is one of the few places on the planet where you might say yes. But North America?

You see my driving point is that this sickly value dominoes into the acceptance of supporting, supplying and even being involved in foreign wars and skirmishes You may disagree if you wish, but it seems to me to be a basic value that has been extrapolated, either consciously, subconsciously or unconsciously into a grosser product of acceptance of human pogroms and mass killings by superior weapons in distant conflagrations between warring sides of various political, religious or racial colours. My view!

What's to be done? Difficult if not a near impossible task… but we need to start somewhere. Education of our kids is a primer. Identifying all the Mr Bigs of the global armaments production and trade is another. Honesty in relation to the root cause of wars might also help (particularly where minerals, oil and gas or other resources can be identified).

Note: having suggested that this is the lowest denominator in capitalism let my reader be reminded that China, a bespoke communist country, is also a major player in arms sales around the world.

Chemical agents that are key ingredients for explosives, landmines, grenades and even poison gas are also to be had from dealers bypassing international agreements and protocols. These basic starter chemicals are mass produced in the civilised West but have still found their way into the hands of petty dictators and extremist groups. In a digital world one would think this could not happen but sadly it does!

Diverse political groups within a single sovereign state that wish the overthrow of the status quo regime should not be supported militarily from outside. Currently Syria is a prime example where Russia, Europe and North America have all plundered the pie with their thumbs, supporting opposing factions to the near destruction and total collapse of that state. In excess of half a million killed in five years with five million having already left, placing enormous stress and strains on neighbouring countries as well as Germany and the European Union generally. Economically, the profits of the warlords in their armament sales to maintain this war pale into insignificance when compared to the total cost of reparation. But then the warlords won't be paying for the necessary final reparation... it will be the suckers paying taxes... sorry, that'll be you and I!

But no war in the history of humankind has ever made economic sense to the masses!

It might seem a feeble aim, but I just wish to assist all countries, especially our rich and powerful friends to grasp the nettle of sensibility, morality and correct decision making to pull back from the precipice of human annihilation and take a new road to omni-inclusive prosperity and safety in a future world society.

Tom Law
Tongio West, Australia. July 2016

The Second Amendment to the United States Constitution: The Second Amendment (Amendment II) to the United States Constitution protects the right of the people to keep and bear arms and was adopted on December 15, 1791, as part of the first ten amendments contained in the Bill of Rights.

The Supreme Court of the United States has ruled that the right belongs to individuals, while also ruling that the right is not unlimited and does not prohibit all regulation of either firearms or similar devices. State and local governments are limited to the same extent as the federal government from infringing this right per the incorporation of the Bill of Rights.

The Second Amendment was based partially on the right to keep and bear arms in English common-law and was influenced by the English Bill of Rights of 1689. Sir William Blackstone described this right as an auxiliary right, supporting the natural rights of self-defence, resistance to oppression, and the civic duty to act in concert in defence of the state. The statement in the English Bill of Rights concerning the right to bear arms is often quoted only in the passage where it is written and not in its full context. In its full context it is clear that the bill was asserting the right of Protestant citizens not to be disarmed by the King without the consent of Parliament and was merely restoring rights to Protestants that the previous King (James II) briefly and unlawfully had removed. In its full context:

> "Whereas the late King James the Second by the Assistance of diverse evill Councellors Judges and Ministers imployed by him did endeavour to subvert and extirpate the Protestant Religion and the Lawes and Liberties of this Kingdome *(list of grievances included...)* ... by causing severall good Subjects being Protestants to be disarmed at the same time when Papists were both Armed and Imployed contrary to Law, *(Recital regarding the change of monarch)* ... thereupon the said Lords Spirituall and Temporall and Commons pursuant to their respective Letters and Elections being now assembled in a full and free Representative of this Nation takeing into their most serious Consideration the best meanes for attaining the Ends aforesaid Doe in the first place (as their Auncestors in like Case have usually done) for the Vindicating and Asserting their ancient Rights and Liberties, Declare *(list of rights included...)* ... That the Subjects which are Protestants may have Arms for their Defence suitable to their Conditions and as allowed by Law"

As passed by the Congress and preserved in the National Archives, with the rest of the original hand-written copy of the Bill of Rights prepared by scribe William Lambert:

A well regulated Militia, being necessary to the security of a free State, the right of the people to keep and bear Arms, shall not be infringed.

As ratified by the States and authenticated by Thomas Jefferson, then Secretary of State:

16

A well regulated militia being necessary to the security of a free state, the right of the people to keep and bear arms shall not be infringed.

It is with this important statement written into American law that the National Rifle Association, its affiliates and many of the general public adheres to i.e that the people have the right to bear arms (i.e carry a weapon). Despite the statistics on brutality in the country, this powerful lobby group (along with the armaments manufacturers and sales outlets) have resisted strong and necessary changes to gun laws and the second amendment in particular. Therein remains the problem for American society and indeed extrapolated to the global community!

It is of significance that the second amendment was written and adopted in 1791. Significant in that the guns at that time were nothing more than toys when compared to the availability of those on the market today. Admittedly one cannot own a modern military style machine gun or possess a Howitzer in ones backyard. However there is still a wide range of automatic and semiautomatic weapons available legally in America. Sadly, there is also a black market for illegal weapons.

The NRA is/was a strong criticizer of Barack Obama and his attempts to tighten gun laws. Some of their pusillanimous outpourings are disgusting and degrading. The NRA and affiliate organizations pander to both the right and the extreme right in America and are self indulgent in their personal rights in what might be described as lunacy and a complete disregard for the mores and values of a modern 21st century society. Their catch cry has always been "Keeping America Safe" and has been repeated often by highly placed civic leaders and politicians in an almost childlike fashion. I say childlike as their psyche hasn't really left the period of 'cowboys and Indians' and their desire is to kill native animals and sometimes humans (by accident or intent) under the pretext of "protecting property and family against criminals, terrorists and murderers". This attitude does not present a problem for America alone, but, through its media (TV and film), has created a diaspora of like-mindedness throughout the world!

But the NRA has not contributed to this world state of affairs by itself. Hollywood has a lot to answer for. The armament manufacturers are at most to blame as they are the ugly profiteers in human misery.

But, you cry, it is not that simple... what about the terrorists, the communists and fascist régimes around the world? Whilst I acknowledge this argument to some extent, even all these groups require money and a supplier of arms. The sad truth is that arms may be readily had from at least one third of the nations of the world! And in the majority of cases, they have no qualms where they are going to. It is a business and warehouses must be emptied!

Here are some gems from the NRA:

"Obama has fully abandoned the pretense that he cares about unifying the nation around shared values and goals. Instead, he is pursuing a nakedly ideological agenda. He claims to be acting in the interest of public safety, but by the most reliable measures we have, the American public is already as safe from violent crime as it's ever been."

"Polls from late 2015 showed soaring support for Second Amendment freedom. In October, a clear majority (56 percent) said they believe

America would be safer if more Americans lawfully carried concealed weapons. The NRA's favorability rating climbed to 58 percent that same month, its highest level in 10 years."

"How did the American people react to gun control's defeat in 2013? Did they storm the Capitol demanding Congress see the error of its ways? Hardly! History records that you instead stormed the polls during the 2014 midterm elections and dealt yet another blow to the anti-gun forces by increasing pro-gun majorities in both houses of Congress. It's a good thing you did!"

"We can't trust anti-gun politicians to respect the Constitution or separation of powers, and when it comes to the Second Amendment, we can't trust that judges will be available or willing to rein in such abuse when it occurs. Our best hope, then, is to ensure they never get the chance by keeping them out of office in the first place."

"Just after the San Bernardino, California, terrorist murders, Sheriff Van Blarcum publicly asked all his deputies to carry (a weapon) while off-duty. On Facebook he wrote: In light of recent events that have occurred in the United States and around the world I want to encourage citizens of Ulster County who are licensed to carry a firearm to please do so…. I want my deputies armed at all times. We are there to protect and serve whether on duty or off."

The officer also said that the anti-gun commentators exhibited depravity and vileness, often full of hate! Rationality seemed to come only from the pro-gun side of the debate?

"People who chose to carry are typically into guns, so they shoot more and are probably even better with their weapons than most cops are."

Sheriff Van Blarcum added: "In my 40 years in law enforcement I've never had to arrest a person with a concealed-carry permit for using their handgun unlawfully. These are good people. It makes sense to ask them to help."

"We're partners with the public in crime prevention... this is increasingly the case because more citizens are getting concealed-carry permits than ever before."

Interesting that seven of the fifty states now have "permitless carry" (also known as "constitutional carry") laws that do not require law-abiding citizens to acquire a permit to practice their right to keep and bear arms. In the US today, those citizens with Right-to-Carry permits outnumber police officers across the country by about 17-to-1! Since 2007, the CPRC found that permits for women have increased by 270 percent while permits for men increased by 156 percent.

Florida's Brevard County Sheriff said: "The only thing that stops a bad guy with a gun is a good guy with a gun. If you're a person who is legally licensed to carry a firearm, now is the time more than ever to realize that you, and you alone, may very well be the first line of defense for you and your family."

Another county Sherriff said: "The government has already said they can't keep track of all these home-grown terrorists, so we can't be everywhere at the same time, so people have to be able to defend themselves. Simply calling 911 and waiting is no longer your best option. You could beg for mercy from a violent criminal, hide under the bed or you could fight back. But are you prepared? Consider taking a certified safety course on handling a firearm so you can defend yourself until we get there."

"Anti-gun politicians and gun-haters in the so-called mainstream media have repeatedly claimed that armed citizens present absolutely no deterrent to violent crime. Who should you believe: Those who know nearly nothing about guns and self-defense, or top county law enforcement officers who strap on a gun every day and head for the streets to keep Americans safe?"

It is not difficult to see where this is all going. According to the NRA the anti-gun lobby is stupid or vile or just plain ignorant. Armed police and armed citizens are the champions of freedom and safety. America is full of potential criminals, killers, terrorists, rapists, thieves and other nasty types so a hidden handgun is an essential item for everyday survival. I am wondering how they lead the world in science, technology, space, astrophysics and a host of other firsts. I cannot get my head around this confronting contradiction about American society.

It seems that the top priority of gun manufacturers and retailers is essentially to maintain a culture of fear in America where every stranger is a potential criminal and murderer. This is a sad indictment on a supposedly modern and informed society!

I have walked the poorer streets of New York and San Francisco and whilst feeling uncomfortable at times have never felt the need for a concealed pistol. To be frank, I find the gun-wearing police officer intimidating and somewhat overbearing in attitude. I think a society where everyone is carrying a gun is a society with a distressing level of constant stress and deep fear. I perceive that there are many movies and TV soap operas that continue to invoke and instil fear into the hearts of both children and adults that soak up the propaganda of "strangers are dangers!" mentality. When Americans visit New Zealand, Australia or the UK they seem to be far less stressed and soon start to enjoy a freedom that they have lost in their homeland. I hate to say it, but the biggest problem for America and the foisting of this problem on the rest of the world is in fact THE SECOND AMENDMENT! This is Tom Law's analysis and opinion.

America's pro-gun lobby group, the National Rifle Association, has posted a video drawing parallels between Australia's 1990s gun buyback scheme and current efforts to tighten firearms laws in the US.

NRA warns the introduction of an Australian-style gun buyback scheme would mean "bans and confiscations" for American gun owners.

The video, which uses Australian newspaper articles from the 1990s, draws mixed reaction on social media... Shooters Union Queensland maintains the 20-year-old information used in the video is still relevant.

Repeatedly the NRA video warns that implementing a similar gun buyback scheme to Australia would mean "bans and confiscations" for American gun owners.

The then Prime Minister John Howard banned semi-automatic rifles and shotguns and the government destroyed more than 600,000 weapons in the buyback scheme. The laws remain in place today. "Never been more proud to live in Australia where we can see past our own blind self-interest and accept regulations that are for the good of the nation" one commenter wrote. When you look at the atrocities committed with firearms in the US it's hard to argue that their system is working, but that's a matter for the US to decide!

NRA supporters also had their say on the video, with one viewer writing: "Never listen to those who are not citizens of the USA. Many of them are just jealous of our freedoms and our gun rights that are protected under our constitution."

And a famous woman also joins the debate:

Dana Loesch is a self-proclaimed 'conservatarian' (?) who hosts a nationally syndicated daily radio show, The Dana Show. She is a regular contributor to Fox News, ABC, CNN and other news shows. A former newspaper columnist and blogger, Loesch penned the best-selling book *'Hands Off My Gun: Defeating the Plot to Disarm America'* in 2014. She co-founded the tea party movement in St. Louis and speaks frequently on the subject of gun control and grassroots.

I find it most disagreeable to see such a woman defending the right for all Americans to carry. I have the gut feeling that a clear majority of women, particularly mothers are not of the Annie Oakley mould! *American Mothers Against Guns* is what I would expect in light of recent deaths. A sex strike might work better than immediately trying to rewrite the law!

Denial of Conjugal Rights

The most famous example of a sex strike was that depicted by the Greek playwright Aristophanes in his play *Lysistrata*, an anti-war comedy. The female characters in the play, led by the eponymous Lysistrata, withheld sex from their husbands as part of their strategy to secure peace and end the Peloponnesian War (431-404 BC). Wives of prolific gun owners might do the same until they get rid of their phallus extensions. I'm sure that for most, their manhood will not be compromised in any way. But maybe not for all!

[Also see controversial hypothesis known as the *'Female Cosmetic Coalitions'*, believed to have played an important role in the development of human civilizations!]

In conclusion it seems that bringing about sensible gun control and sensible laws in America are doomed to failure whilst the Second Amendment and the all pervasive gun culture of its citizens prevail. But as aforementioned this also has a direct unpleasant influence on the rest of the world. Weapon manufacturers are making lots of money. They also have persuasive political clout. As with tobacco, alcohol and drug usage, society is struggling for some sense of normality and well being without the shadow of fear and sterility. Our TV screens are saturated with both fictional and real life true events of horrific proportions. I do not condone censorship but less violence and graphic horror together with a society where guns are limited would seem to be a worthwhile goal. Those pushing wheelbarrows of conspiracy theories and plots to disarm citizens, in my opinion, are the sick members of society requiring mental health treatment.

The person that wishes to go to the forest and hunt wild animals where those animals are in excessive numbers for the environment, I can accept. The farmer that has too many rabbits, foxes or other rodents, I have sympathy for. The person that wishes to join a club and attend a shooting range for practice and skill building, I can understand.

But the housewife carrying a loaded pistol in her handbag at the supermarket, I cannot accept.

The man on the street with a concealed gun I can neither accept.

The farmer with dozens of rifles in his house I do not accept.

The sporting hunter owning dozens of rifles I cannot accept.

Automatic and even some semiautomatic weapons should never be in the hands of citizens, nor military style weapons.

All pistol owners should belong to a recognised club where his or her weapon is stored in a safe for use at the club premises.

Rifle owners should be restricted to two weapons. Both the weapon and the owner to be registered with the appropriate authority.

The acquisition of guns should be severely restricted. Free markets and gun swaps should be outlawed as should third party salespersons.

Collector's pieces should be *non-functional* as a fire arm.

Severe penalties need to be revised to ensure that gun laws are met.

The alternatives we know to be the status quo with the continuation and likely inflation of the horrific statistics of gun deaths. I consider freedom as a place where I can be without the fear of other citizens carrying concealed guns. This is my value.

NSSF: **National Shooting Sports Foundation** is the trade association for America's firearms industry.

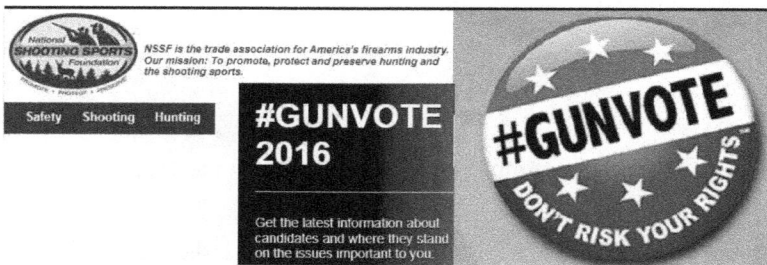

Quotes from their website:

Statement on the Passing of Senior US Supreme Court Associate Justice Antonin Scalia:

"On behalf of our members, the National Shooting Sports Foundation wishes to express deep sadness on the passing of Senior Associate

Supreme Court Justice Antonin Scalia while on a hunting trip. Justice Scalia authored the pivotal Heller decision and was a true champion of Americans' right to keep and bear arms. Our thoughts are with his family and friends. A man of rare wit, scholarship and wisdom, he will always stand tall in our memories."

Girl Power

The number of women hunters, target shooters and gun owners has increased dramatically since the start of the new millennium. A new NSSF infographic gives a quick look at one of the fastest-growing segments of the shooting sports.

What can I say about the National Shooting Sports Foundation other than it is an organization with the sole purpose of promulgating the continuation of gun sales for the profit of the gun manufacturers. I am uncertain as to whether it has any social consciousness and consequently merits no further comment from me!

And then there is the: 'American Firearms Institute'. The following is taken from their website:

"Established to provide accurate and balanced information, resources on guns and the second amendment. Gun history, advice to the beginner, safety, statistics, manufacturers, gun laws, legislation, plus a *Gun Dealer and Gun Manufacturer Directory*. Please explore our site and learn as much as you can.

The main sources of gun crime are:

1. Inner City cycles of violence and gangs
2. Violent Criminals
3. Mental health problems associated, most often, with the use of alcohol and drugs. Sometimes involving the lack of use of prescribed drugs

Gun crimes are not caused by:

- Legal gun owners
- Guns

American Firearms Philosophy -

Introduction

Firearm ownership is a Constitutional Right of every American guaranteed by the Second Amendment of the US Constitution, ratified on December 15, 1791. It proves the foresight of our founding fathers in providing us with the freedom to choose to own a firearm or not. American Firearms Institute supports that guarantee. American Firearms Institute (AFI) supports that choice.

Enough with the laws already:

There are safe guards in place to ensure that gun owners meet certain criteria before receiving possession of a firearm; these include passing a background and criminal check. Felons and domestic violence perpetrators are not allowed to own firearms. Mental health issues are taken into consideration in applying, as are addictions to alcohol and drugs. The penalty for knowingly filling in a firearm application form incorrectly is 10 years in prison.

It's the Criminal:

There are an estimated 280 million firearms in the US - all owned by law abiding citizens. There is no record of the number of illegal guns that exist. The criminally minded laugh at society's gun control laws, according to an FBI report issued in March of 2007, which you will find under the *Report's* section of the site.

Criminals find it amusing that laws are passed that are assumed will make any difference to them and their way of living. Criminals by their nature are anti-social with sociopath or psychopathic tendencies. They never purchase their firearms through legal channels or abide by laws. Many have no qualms at shooting at their victim or killing a police officer. Why? Because they're criminals! The law does not apply to them until they get caught. And then it's too late.

There is vast disconnect in the equating of gun ownership and criminal behavior. Certain members of society- the anti-gun groups- automatically equate gun ownership with criminal activity. And for that reason they want firearms removed from society altogether.

A does not equal B. Their reasoning defies logic.

Firearms have been in existence for 700+ years- the first reference to the use of gunpowder in Europe dates from 1247. The first record in China dates from 142 CE. It would be easier to suggest that we all stop breathing than attempt to rid the world of firearms. Why? Because for most societies they are a source for achieving and holding power. Ownership dictates how countries are run, how wars are won and how lives are lived and lost. Firearms are not going anywhere.

Power to the People:

Our forefathers framed out our constitution to ensure that the power of the populace remained in the hands of the people. To ensure that, (this is a matter of much debate) they ensured that we would have the means available to us to counter any tyrannical efforts to rule us. Thus the Second Amendment came into being. It also gave us the power to choose whether to own a firearm or not. An individual choice.

Who owns the guns?

There are three categories of firearm owners in the USA:

1. The government, represented by the military and law enforcement.
2. Private citizen owners who legally possess 280 million firearms.
3. Criminals.

Which of these is the source of criminal firearm activity? The last, of course. The proof is in the news everyday and our prisons are filled to capacity with them. Why then are the members of category 2, private citizen owners, being attacked for legal possession of firearms? There is no link factually or otherwise between legal firearm ownership and criminality. None whatsoever!"

... and so it goes on. But we have enough here to see some errors of logic in the philosophy of the American Firearms Institute!

- Firstly they don't mention any restrictions on the number of firearms any single person is permitted to own. So we can only assume that this number is as much as anyone desires!
- Secondly, they fail to recognize any possible crossover from a responsible citizen to a mentally disturbed citizen or criminal... they assume these groups of people to be eternally mutually exclusive!
- They do not address the 'ease of acquisition' of firearms in the US. Gun markets, private sales, deceased estates and even loony offspring!
- The second amendment, which they cling to feverishly, was written in the 18th century and that is where it belongs! The writers could not foresee the sophistication of modern rifles, handguns and automatic weapons, now a tyrannical menace to society per se. The second amendment also carries an understanding that the people may rise up as an armed group to oppose tyranny in a revolutionary way.
- It is not guns that are the problem? I covered this in my last point. Many so called legal gun owners have proven to be irresponsible leading to deaths. For instance the child in the supermarket trolley that takes a loaded pistol from his/her mother's handbag. The teenage son that borrows his father's semiautomatic and goes on a shooting rampage at school.
- It is assumed that all guns are to be removed from society. Tom advocates that hand gun owners must belong to a club or

31

association where the guns are kept. He also believes that there remains a place for recreational hunting with rifles/shotguns to a limit and under certain controls. He does believe that it is possible to have a society where not every police officer is carrying a sidearm; only special and particular officers need these!

- It fails to recognize that guns and the armament industries are not primarily there to uphold the second amendment but rather to make handsome profits for owners and shareholders. This (to Tom's mind) is the dark side of unrestrained and rampant capitalism!

- There is an ongoing failure of the whole of society to control the final resting place of guns when they are of no further use to the owner due to death, old age or some form of incapacity. The number of weapons currently held by citizens is closer to 400 million, far in excess of those legally registered!

- Fails to recognize (by its absence and non-discussion) the statistic of in excess, now, of 10000 annual deaths from guns in America (and this excludes almost as many again by so called suicides by gun!)

President Obama has tried to address the outrageous statistics of deaths in America by guns of various descriptions. The recent White Paper (released in Jan 2016 and provided in the Appendices) makes various suggestions for tighter gun control in an effort to diminish greatly the unnecessary and tragic deaths of so many citizens. The various organizations mentioned above have whipped up a massive outpouring of hysteria to block the intentions of a most sensible paper. They shout that their rights are being quashed in an unreasonable and undemocratic

32

fashion. They go to ridiculous lengths to prove that murderers and terrorists need to be confronted by the average citizen with his Glock at the ready, like some Roy Rogers or Hopalong Cassidy of a bygone era. If the madness of mass killings and the continuation of thousands of gun related deaths annually are to be resolved, it can only be achieved by a *deletion of the second amendment from the constitution*. Alternatively, all the misery and sad loss of future American lives must jointly be the responsibility of all the above lobby groups, the manufacturers as well as the perpetrators.

There is evidence of progress in gun control however:

> Heller v. District of Columbia, Civil Action No. 08-1289 (RMU), No. 23., 25 On March 26, 2010, the D.C. Circuit denied the follow up appeal of Dick Heller who requested the court to overturn the new District of Columbia gun control ordinances newly enacted after the 2008 Heller ruling. The court refused to do so, stating that the firearms registration procedures; the prohibition on assault weapons; and the prohibition on large capacity ammunition feeding devices were found *to not violate the Second Amendment*. On September 18, 2015, the D.C. Circuit ruled that requiring gun owners to re-register a gun every three years, make a gun available for inspection or pass a test about firearms laws violated the Second Amendment. The court upheld requirements that gun owners be fingerprinted, photographed and complete a safety training course.

There have also been laws passed restricting ownership to juveniles, mentally impaired persons, persons convicted of violent crime (including domestic violence) and various other criminal offences. However, there is no semblance of uniformity across all the states which have brought along inevitable problems in gun supply. Postal and Internet sales have not been curbed either.

As said repeatedly in this book, the Second Amendment and the American psyche regarding gun ownership has consequences internationally also, influencing peoples and nations far beyond the shores of America!

Gun Manufacturers and Suppliers

Russia delivered 10,000 Kalashnikov rifles, along with millions of rounds of ammunition, to the Afghan government as part of a security agreement between the two nations (Feb 2016). The rifles were delivered at a ceremony at Kabul's military airport. "The respected government of Russia has provided weapons along with its ammunition to our Afghan forces that they needed," said Afghan national security adviser, Mohammad Hanif Atmar. "They have provided this at a very crucial time to our Afghan police force and other security organizations." Russia's ambassador in Kabul, Alexander Mantytskiy, said his country is committed to helping the Afghans and the Afghan forces combat problems like terrorism and drugs.

My comment is that the Russian manufacturing firms suddenly found their warehouses full of these weapons and not to be outdone by America, the Government has again waded politically into Afghan affairs. Perhaps there has been a temporary pause in black market sales to the various third world governments along with revolutionary and terrorist organisations. As supplies of other weapons were becoming excessive in number and also outdated, it was expedient to join Al Assad's war in Syria and defray warehouse stocks by sending missiles and bombs to just about anyone on the ground. But hey… everyone has been bombing Syria with only Assad's forces and the Kurds fighting IS on the ground with troops. But even the Kurds are finding it hard as Turkey wishes to bomb them now. One suspects Sunni Saudi and Turkey have each blood on their hands with covert support for IS in the past! What a mess!

But let us not get too embroiled here on the details and various groups involved in that sad war. I want to focus more on the manufacturers and suppliers of armaments that keep the economics and profits of war turning over!

I even theorise that the Falklands war way back in the 1970s was tweaked to some degree in Argentina by rogue secret service agents i.e the *idea* of an invasion was psychologically injected into the military and political minds of Argentineans at the time (somehow groomed) so that profits in arms sales could be made and others tested! No? Well it would be difficult to prove other than a serious in-depth look at the armament manufacturers' account books! (French, American, British and others!)

List of American Gun Manufacturers:

Accu-Tek Firearms

Advanced Armament Corp

Armalite   (makes AR-15, AR-180 and AR-10 Rifles)

Arsenal Firearms

AYA, Aguirre y Aranzabal

Benelli

Bersa

Boberg Arms Corp

Brenneke USA

Bushmaster

Cabot Gun Co

Caesar Guerini

Century Arms

Charles Daly

Chiappa Firearms

Christensen Arms

Cobra Firearms

Coonan

Dillon Aero

Franchi

Glock

Henry Repeating Rifles

Hi-Point

Kel-Tec-Cnc

Knight Rifle

Llama

Marlin Firearms Co

Mossberg

Olympic Arms

Red Jacket Firearms

Rossi Firearms

SAKO

SigArms

Springfield Armory

Taurus

Traditions Firearms:

Walther

Winchester Guns

Adcor Defense

American Derringer

American Tactical Imports

Arsenal Inc

Auto-Ordnance Corp

Barret

Beretta

Blaser

Bond Arms

Browning

C&H Precision Weapons

Cadillac Gage   (owned by Textron)

Calico

Ceska Zbrojavka

Charter Arms

Chipmunk Rifles

Cimarron Arms

Colt   (main producer of M16 an M4)

Cooper Firearms

Connecticut Valley Arms

Dakota Arms

FN Herstal

Freedom Arms

Heckler Koch

High Standard Co.

Ithaca Gun Company

Kimber

Legacy Sports

Magnum Research

McMillan Firearms

North American Arms

Para-Ordnance

Guns Manufactured by Para-Ordnance

Remington Firearms

Ruger Firearms

Savage Arms

Smith & Wesson (largest producer of handguns in the United States)

Stoeger

Thompson Center Arms

Vincenzo Bernardelli

Weatherby

.... and some more:

Christensen Arms

Cobra Firearms (compact handguns for personal protection)

Daisy Manufacturing Company, Inc.

Dillon Precision

Edward Arms Company

European American Armory Corp.

G. L. Jones (reproduction colonial firearms, flintlocks, and fowlers)

Heckler & Koch, Inc. (US subsidiary)

Heritage Manufacturing, Inc.

Kahr Arms (compact semi-auto pistols designed for concealed carry)

Kimber of America

LaserMax (laser gun sights)

Lazzeroni Arms Company

Marlin Rifle

Mauser-Werke Oberndorf

MTM Case-Gard   (shooting sports accessories)

North American Arms, Inc.

O.F. Mossberg

Ronald Wharton Riflemaker

SIG Arms   (for military, law enforcement, security agencies, self-defense)

SKB Shotguns

Springfield Armory

SSK Industries

Sturm, Ruger and Company (NYSE:RGR)

Valkyrie Arms, Ltd. (semi-automatic versions of classic military machine guns)

Vector Arms

Weatherby Firearms

Wilson Combat

Winchester Rifles and Shotguns

ZDF Import/Export, Inc. (Importer of VEPR Rifle -based on Kalashnikov series)

The whole fabric of American society is interwoven with the sediments of capitalism: racketeering, big business, hidden money trails, corruption and the placement of profit above the values of society. If this were not true, we would not see the all too frequent horrific mass killings of innocents on the streets, in the shopping malls and even in business offices. The flow of arms from many of the above manufacturers to members of the public seems to continue in unwanted excess despite regulations and laws. The lobby groups are merely the mouthpieces of the executives and shareholders of these companies. Money over sanity!

This seems so contradictory to all the great things from America: high standards of technology and medicine; creativity in agricultural and bio sciences; discoveries in astronomy, physics and the space sciences; computing and computer networks; leaders in film, the arts and literature... the list goes on. So why this 'other' obsession on 'Keeping America Safe' ? Is it a part of the philosophy 'invent the disease' followed up quickly by 'invent the cure and make a buck' ?

In the long run it is the people that must decide. Protest to the system: the Congress and Senate, the judges, courts and the rule of law. Reason over emotion. Something fundamental needs to change in order to halt and prevent further carnage on a grand scale. A factory that makes guns can be altered and tweaked to a factory making useful things for society at home or abroad.

"Ah yes, Glock... they are a brilliant manufacturer of electric engines in the new age!"

"Winchester you say? Ah yes, a fantastic producer of fishing rods and farm fence materials... a massive exporter!"

"Mauser-Werke Oberndorf ? Ah yes, one of the world's leaders in building construction and design... even built that new Moon Hotel you know!"

"Ruger? Ah yes, one of the biggest in sporting and gymnasium equipment... has a dozen factories in China alone!"

So what will the future hold? What will be the lasting indictment and legacy for all these companies by the end of the 21st century?

An epitaph of great works for society

OR

The recorded prime contributors to the death of millions of citizens?

But some of these manufacturers are also related to the producers of military hardware for home and abroad. We will move on to these in a later chapter.

Explosive Materials Suppliers

Semtex: Semtex is a general-purpose plastic explosive containing RDX and PETN. It is used in commercial blasting, demolition, and in certain military applications. Semtex became notoriously popular with terrorists because it was, until recently, extremely difficult to detect.

PETN is a component of the plastic explosive (Semtex-H) chemically named pentaerythritol tetranitrate. Plastic explosive Semtex is a type of grenade containing C4 that sticks to the first surface it touches, including other players, before exploding.

On May 25, 1997, Bohumil Šole, a scientist often said to have been involved with inventing Semtex, strapped the explosive to his body and committed suicide in the Priessnitz spa of Jeseník, Czech Republic. Semtex is now widely used in military explosives by Government armed forces across the world as well as a favoured component of bombs, landmines and grenades manufactured for and by terrorist groups.

Composition of Semtex

Compound	Semtex 1A	Semtex H	Semtex 2P
PETN	76%	40.9%	58.45%
RDX	4.6%	41.2%	22.9%
binder styrene-butadiene	9.4%	9%	9.2%
plasticizer n-octyl phthalate, tributyl citrate	9%	7.9%	8.45%
antioxidant N-phenyl-2-naphthylamine	0.5%	0.5%	0.5%
Dye	0.5% Sudan IV (reddish brown to red)	0.5% Sudan I (red-orange to yellow)	(brown)

Semtex was invented in the late 1950s by Stanislav Brebera, a chemist at VCHZ Synthesia, Czech Republic. The explosive is named after Semtín, a suburb of Pardubice where the mixture was first manufactured in 1964. The plant was later renamed to become Explosia. Semtex was very similar to other plastic explosives, especially C-4, in being easily malleable but usable over a greater temperature range. It stays plastic between −40 and +60 °C and is also waterproof. While C-4 is off-white in colour, Semtex is red or brick-orange.

The new explosive was widely exported, notably to the government of North Vietnam, which received 14 tonnes during the Vietnam War. However, the main consumer was Libya- about 700 tonnes of Semtex were exported to Libya between 1975 and 1981 by Omnipol, a company based in Prague specialising in the trading of defence and aerospace equipment.

It has also been used by Islamic militants in the Middle East and by the Provisional Irish Republican Army (IRA) and the Irish National Liberation Army in Northern Ireland.

Exports fell after the name became closely associated with terrorist attacks. Export of Semtex was progressively tightened and since 2002 all of Explosia's sales have been controlled by a government ministry. As of 2001, only approximately 10 tonnes of Semtex were produced annually, almost all for domestic use. In response to international agreements, Semtex has a detection tag added to produce a distinctive signature to aid detection of its source.

A dozen favoured explosives, including TNT, RDX, HMX, PETN, TATB, and HNS, dominate current weaponizable explosive formulations. It is said that the largest application of explosives is mining. However this statement excludes warehouse stocks that military organisations hold in almost every country just waiting to be applied in wars! Most commercial explosives are organic compounds containing NO_2, $-ONO_2$ and $-NHNO_2$ groups that, when detonated, release gases and enormous amounts of heat energy causing deadly high pressure shock waves creating physical destruction of objects in their path.

A detonator which is certain to prime the explosive to a sustained and continuous detonation is necessary. Reference is made to the Sellier-Bellot scale that consists of detonators from 1 to 10, each of which corresponds to an increasing charge weight. In practice, most explosives on the market today are sensitive to an 8 detonator, where the charge is equivalent to 2 grams of mercury fulminate (an explosive chemical).

Examples of primary high explosives used as detonators include:

- Acetone peroxide
- Alkali metal ozonides
- Ammonium permanganate
- Ammonium chlorate
- Azidotetrazolates
- Azo-clathrates
- Benzoyl peroxide

46

- Benzvalene
- Chlorine oxides
- Copper(I) acetylide
- Copper(II) azide
- Cumene hydroperoxide
- Cyanogen azide
- Diacetyl peroxide
- 1-Diazidocarbamoyl-5-azidotetrazole
- Diazodinitrophenol
- Diazomethane
- Diethyl ether peroxide
- 4-Dimethylaminophenylpentazole
- Disulfur dinitride
- Ethyl azide
- Explosive antimony
- Fluorine perchlorate
- Fulminic acid
- Halogen azides:

    -Fluorine azide

    -Chlorine azide

    -Bromine azide

- Hexamethylene triperoxide diamine
- Hydrazoic acid
- Hypofluorous acid
- Lead azide
- Lead styphnate
- Lead picrate

- Manganese heptoxide
- Mercury(II) fulminate
- Mercury nitride
- Methyl ethyl ketone peroxide
- Nitrogen trihalides:

  -Nitrogen trichloride

  -Nitrogen tribromide

  -Nitrogen triiodide

- Nitroglycerine
- Nitronium perchlorate
- Nitrotetrazolate-N-oxides
- Octaazacubane
- Pentazenium hexafluoroarsenate
- Peroxy acids
- Peroxymonosulfuric acid
- Selenium tetraazide
- Silicon tetraazide
- Silver azide
- Silver acetylide
- Silver fulminate
- Silver nitride
- Sodium azide
- Tellurium tetraazide
- *tert*-Butyl hydroperoxide

The legality of possessing or using explosives varies by jurisdiction; various countries around the world have enacted explosives laws and require licenses to manufacture, distribute, store, use, possess explosives or their ingredients. Shipping labels and tags may include both United Nations and national markings.

United Nations markings include numbered 'Hazard Class' and 'Division (HC/D)' codes and alphabetic 'Compatibility Group' codes. Though the two are related, they are separate and distinct. Any Compatibility Group designator can be assigned to any Hazard Class and Division. Examples of national markings include for example United States Department of Transportation codes.

Explosives warning signs: The Hazard Class and Division (HC/D) of the United Nations is a numeric designator within a hazard class indicating the character, predominance of associated hazards, and potential for causing personnel casualties and property damage. It is an internationally accepted system that communicates, using the minimum amount of markings, the primary hazard associated with a substance.
e.g 1.1 Mass Detonation Hazard- a class 1 explosive
An explosion will sympathetically detonate the surrounding items. The explosion could propagate to all or the majority of the items stored together, causing a mass detonation.

Despite all this legalese regarding storage, shipping, manufacture etc. we see that the Czech Republic, for example, produced tonnes of Semtex that found its way to terrorist organisations. Further, international companies, despite supposedly careful stock takes and control of sales are still manufacturing weapons grade explosives that find their way to unstable regimes and even terrorist organisations. As per usual it is the *money trail and profit* that is the prime executioner of innocent people around the world where aggressive wars are taking place. Some powerful Governments unashamedly permit their armed forces to experiment or demonstrate their military capabilities in these minor conflicts. A disgusting example was Putin's Russia demonstrating its missile fire power from warships in the Black Sea into Syria in early 2016 striking civilian populations ... a war crime in my book necessitating prosecution!

What is the Explosives Manufacturing Industry?

These industries comprise companies that manufacture explosives. The main product grouping is commercial explosives, including ammonium nitrate based explosives. Other products covered include initiating systems (detonators), propellants, pyrotechnic products (fireworks and flares) and explosives produced for use by the military. Industry participants may also produce blasting accessories such as blasting and detonating caps, fuses and cords, and detonators and safety fuses.

Explosive Manufacturers:

AEL Mining Services Limited - Manufacturer and supplier of commercial explosives, initiating systems, blasting solutions and services in Africa to the mining, quarrying and construction industry.

Applied Explosives Technology - Explosives for mining, engineering and pyrotechnics for the film, television and advertising industries.

Armag Corporation - Manufacturer of storage products for arms, ammunition, explosives and blasting agents.

Blasters Tool and Supply Co., Inc., - Blasting and bomb technician accessories for the mining, demolition and law enforcement industries.

Can-Blast - Canadian based manufacturer of pneumatic loading equipment for cartridged emulsion and water gel explosives.

Chamundi Explosives [P] Ltd. - India based manufacturer of safety fuse and gunpowder for blasting operations.

Copperhead Chemical Company - Manufacturer of nitro glycerine for pharmaceutical use and of explosive materials for use in propellants, fuel additives, and munitions applications. Also offers custom nitration services.

Davey Bickford - Complete range of electric and pyrotechnical initiators designed for the automotive, mining and armament industries.

East Coast Powder Magazine - Specializing in custom made magazines for explosives, pyrotechnics and hazardous materials.

Explosives Limited - Explosives distributor, supplying both packaged and bulk explosive products to the industry. Specifications and blasting formulas.

Gillrange Ltd. - Online product catalogue including explosives, blasting agents, security pyrotechnics.

Great Western Corporation - A manufacturer, distributor and exporter of metal relocatable explosives storage magazines.

HG Explosives - Explosives and explosive stores and magazines. Firm based in North Lincolnshire UK.

HiEx Technologies and HiEx Technical Services Ltd. - Manufactures the Teleblaster radio remote blasting system, and drystick dewatering pipes. Consulting to the blasting industry for road construction, quarrying and mining.

Ideal Supply Inc. - Supplier of a full line of blasting, surveying, and safety supplies. Product lines include measuring, surveying, tools, wire, reels, electronics, loading, storage, safety, and organizing equipment.

Instantel - Portable seismographs for controlled blast monitoring, blast analysis and pile driving.

Irish Industrial Explosives - Manufacturers and distributors of explosives and accessories to the Irish mining, quarrying and civil engineering industries.

ISTROCHEM a.s - Explosives manufacturer in Slovakia

Jiangsu Provincial Chemical and Building Material Trading Co.Ltd. - Import and export company of civil explosives and chemicals within the Jiangsu Province, China

Johnson Hi-Tech Explosives - Perth, Western Australia based manufacturer and distributor of innovative explosive solutions and custom explosive solutions.

Kontinitro AG - Manufacturer of Explomet-FO the detonating velocity measuring instrument.

Koryo Explosives Co. Ltd. - Makers of emulan, kinex, prillit detonating cord nped and konel.

Lubrizol - Supplier of PIBSA based invert emulsifiers for use in the production of emulsion explosives.

Nitro-Chem SA - Polish manufacturer of explosives.

Nordex Explosives - Publicly traded manufacturer and distributor of explosives for mining and industrial applications in Kirkland Lake, Ontario. Products information, technical specifications, and investor information. (TSX symbol NXX)

Orica - Supplier of commercial explosives and blasting technology serving markets in North America, Latin America, Europe, Asia and Australia.

Pacific Scientific Energetic Materials Co. - Design, and production of explosives, propellants, and pyrotechnic actuated devices. Lead Azide Replacement, Initiators and Detonators (laser, electric and percussion).

RedBull Powder Company Ltd, Auckland, New Zealand - RedBull Powder Company Ltd is a blasting contractor and supplier of explosives to construction and mining industries. It provides control of environmental effects of blasting, control and reduction of ground vibration, full rock-on-ground service.

Sichuan Hongguang Chemical Co.,Ltd. - Manufacturer of TNT, 2,4-DNT, 80/20-DNT, nitrotulene(p,o,m), 2,5-dimenthylphenol, p-nitrobenzoic acid, phloroglucin, Lomefloxacin Hydrochloride , Doxazosin mesylate tablet, and Cetirizine Hydrochloride. China

Snpe Group - Industrial group specialized in fine derivatives, and in energetic materials (propellant, explosives.)

Sukhdev Explosives Pvt. Ltd. - Supplier and Consultancy provider in India.

Thomas Instruments - Blasting Electronics - Supplier of galvanometers which allow for the checking of stray current when using electric blasting caps.

VALsynthese - Specialist in high risk chemical reactions, compounds and explosives, from Switzerland.

Vetrivel Explosives Pvt Ltd - Industrial explosives manufacturer and exporters from India.

Zukovich Morhard and Wade LLC - Design and engineering company, specializing in explosives identification and emulsion manufacturing projects.

Also:

Platt Bros and Co

Stresau Laboratory Inc

Field Forensics

Mil-Spec Industries Corp

Gun F X Tactical Development Inc

Island Pyrochemical Industries

ACCURATE ENERGETIC SYSTEMS, LLC

Austin Powder Company

DynaEnergetics

Dyno Nobel

GENERAL DYNAMICS ORDNANCE & TACTICAL SYSTEMS --
MUNITIONS SERVICES

Hunting Titan

Maxam North America Inc

MP Associates Inc

Nelson Brothers Inc

Senex Explosives inc

Special Devices Inc

Teledyne Risi Inc

Vet's Explosives

African Explosives

California Powder Works

Ensign-Bickford Company

Explosia a.s.

Hanwha

Joliet Army Ammunition Plant

Laflin & Rand Powder Company

Low Wood Gunpowder Works

Oklahoma Ordnance Works

Oriental Powder Company

Royal Ordnance Factory

Tamil Nadu Industrial Explosives Limited

West Virginia Ordnance Works

… to name but a few!

How does killing commence one might ask? Verbal abuse leading to physical abuse leading to the grasping of a knife or other weapon. This is the order of things in the suburbs between people; sometimes family or friends and sometimes between complete strangers (for example drunken youth outside a nightclub in the early morning hours). Young people with a grudge against a school teacher, fellow students or a police officer... any symbol of authority. A person recently dismissed from her or his employ wishing to take a vendetta against the boss or the boss' family. Acts of maiming or murder are often causal effects of perceived injustice, perpetrated by a disturbed mind. The normal person will adjust and move on.

On a grander scale we see sovereign nations taking a decision to go to war. The causes here are generally more complex and may fall into several categories:

A perceived need to expand territory

A result of some continued aggravation such as border definition, economic unfairness, racial tension

A historical record of antipathy over decades or centuries

A joining with a fellow nation already at war

A perceived threat leading to a 'first strike'

A perceived righteous reason to overthrow a despotic government

A capitalistic venturous invasion for perceived future economic gain (empire building)

A political or religious fabrication perceived as the correct path to right injustice

You might think of more but I think I have covered most here! The one not mentioned of course is the war for the sake of war covertly started by hidden third parties merely to extend and promote the business of producing armaments for profit! At the conclusion of the Second World War aspersions were cast against certain individuals and companies labelled 'war profiteers'! Historically, Governments during war have always required manpower, materials and armaments to carry out the war. In any immediate post-war period, Governments have a necessity to 'rebuild' cities and the entire nation in an effort to bring about a return to normality and civilisation. Growing up in Southeast London during the 1950s, playing on bomb sites was a common thing for children (often away from the eyes of their hard working parents). It is now repeated in many Afghani, Iraqi and Syrian cities!

What I am theorising here, as much as you might throw up your hands in disgust and disbelief, is that the sludge of the capitalistic world now engineers ways and means to create instabilities and create wars merely to swell the coffers of profiteers in all the industries necessary; pre, during and post conflict! After all, states or organisations within states require arms such as explosives, grenades, bombs and automatic weapons to proceed in a war. On a larger scale: fighter planes, missiles, tanks, bigger guns and bombs, ships and submarines. There are also the dirty weapons such as biological agents, chemicals and poisonous gas which require base chemicals and materials to produce. All these require large amounts of money to be procured and a chain of buyers and sellers to reach the market destination. Regardless of who the end users are, the original manufacturers remain the same international giants sailing along their merry way to bigger profits! The guilty will try to extol their righteousness and legality in what they are producing in exclamations such as:

"We only sell to legitimate customers such as representatives of democratic governments"

"There is no evidence that we have ever sold directly to terrorist organisations or totalitarian regimes"

"Smaller illegal companies must be producing copies of our weapons"

"It is not our responsibility or fault if some of our weapons fall into the hands of these groups... there must be some buyers with fake credentials"

"Some once democratic nations have become unstable and have sold on armaments... this is beyond our control!"

... and similar nonsense.

Often the reality and truth is that weapons and munitions build up in warehouses and become out of date. Also, companies make huge profits and contribute in no small way to the economy of certain nations (especially our own), providing employment to hundreds of thousands of workers. Any downturn in manufacturing or extensive period without demand would jeopardise the whole industry and consequently affect the nation's economy.

And then we also have all the support systems during and after the war. Contracts for security, iron, steel, concrete and glass for the rebuilding as well as all the household goods, electronics and a whole host of accessories and materials for the rebuild. Somebody makes money out of all this human misery! Refugees are a strain on most economies but others see them as a respite in an otherwise falling workforce, particularly in stalwart economies with an aging population and having an expansion of industry generally. But I must restate my main proposition here, and that is that *the giant corporations in the armaments business are making huge profits from sales and it is in their interest that wars do not disappear from the planet!*

[I wonder if they are connected to the major providers of books... I have found recently that just about anything written about 'peace' has jumped in price by several hundred percent! Even 'peace studies' is a dirty concept in our schools these days. Probably in the interest again of 'keeping us all safe!']

So who are these dark villains? Let them be brought out into the light of day for all to see and be eternally recognised!

I have already mentioned gun manufacturers in an earlier chapter. Let me discuss the BIG players now:

It is estimated that yearly, over 1.5 trillion United States dollars are spent on military expenditures worldwide (2.7% of World GDP). The combined arms sales of the top 100 largest arms producing companies amounted to an estimated $395 billion in 2012 according to Stockholm International Peace Research Institute (SIPRI). In 2004 over $30 billion were spent in the international arms trade (a figure that excludes domestic sales of arms). According to SIPRI, the volume of international transfers of major weapons in 2010–14 was 16 per cent higher than in 2005–2009. The five biggest exporters* in 2010–14 were the United States, Russia, China, Germany and France, and the five biggest importers were India, Saudi Arabia, China, the United Arab Emirates (UAE) and Pakistan.

The Control Arms Campaign, founded by Amnesty International, Oxfam, and the International Action Network on Small Arms, estimated in 2003 that there were over 639 million small arms in circulation, and that over 1,135 companies based in more than 98

60

different countries manufacture small arms as well as their various components and ammunition. For 2016 the figure would be closer to one billion small arms in circulation!

[* There is some argument here that places Britain ahead of some of these nations!]

Military aircraft (both land-based and naval aviation), conventional missiles and military satellites all form part of the most technologically advanced sector of the market. Prominent aerospace firms include Rolls Royce, BAE, Dassault Aviation, Sukhoi, Mikoyan, EADS, Finmeccanica, Thales Group, Lockheed Martin, Northrop Grumman and Boeing. There are also several multinational consortiums mostly involved in the manufacturing of fighter jets, such as the Eurofighter.

The cyber-security industry is becoming the most important sector of the defence industry as cyber attacks are being deemed as one of the greatest risk to defence in modern times. The major organisations involved in cyber defence are:

- Intel
- Lockheed Martin
- Northrop Grumman
- Raytheon
- The Boeing Company
- General Dynamics

But do not be confused here... Governments are also spending huge amounts of money *developing* skills and software to 'mount' cyber attacks on potential enemies in a war situation or, more unseemly, retaliatory tit-for-tat attacks during peacetime (with the added risk, the potential of starting a war!)

According to the Stockholm International Peace Research Institute, the world's largest suppliers of armaments are:

2014 rank	Supplier	Arms exports ($US millions)
1	United States	10194
2	Russia	5971
3	China	1978 – see below
4	France	1200
5	Germany	1110
6	United Kingdom	1083
7	Israel	1074
8	Spain	824
9	Italy	786
10	Ukraine	664
11	Netherlands	561
12	Sweden	394
13	Switzerland	350
14	Turkey	274
15	Canada	234

China: probably closer to between 5000- 10000 (estimate 2015)

Other sources have suggested that, as of 2008, Britain has become the world's leading developer of arms with the British company BAE Systems. Defence group BAE Systems is the first company outside the United States to reach the top position, thanks to a deal with the Pentagon for mine-resistant vehicles used in Iraq and Afghanistan. According to the Stockholm International Peace Research Institute the former British Aerospace group's arms sales went ahead of American market leaders Lockheed Martin and Boeing. The report reveals BAE's US subsidiary was alone responsible for 61.5% of the group's arms sales and around 58.5% of total group sales. This demonstrates BAE's increasing reliance on orders for conventional weapons as the United States cuts back on its nuclear arsenal. The British figures were also boosted by orders for Eurofighter Typhoon jets from Saudi Arabia.

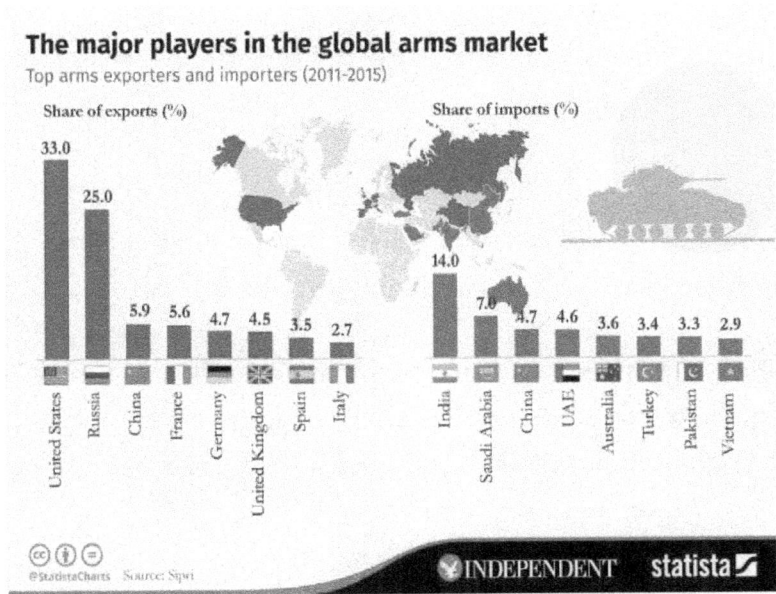

The major players in the global arms market
Top arms exporters and importers (2011-2015)

World's largest weapons importers:

2014 rank	Recipient	Arms imports ($US millions)
1	Saudi Arabia	2629
2	India	1550
3	China	1357

2014 rank	Recipient	Arms imports ($US millions)
4	Indonesia	1200
5	Vietnam	1058
6	Taiwan	1039
7	United Arab Emirates	1031
8	Australia	842
9	Oman	738
10	Singapore	717
11	Pakistan	659
12	Azerbaijan	640
13	Iraq	627
14	Morocco	594

Why does Saudi need all these weapons… because it can afford them? Or perhaps it just wishes to have the best and most up to date?

In 2015 Japan's government approved its largest military budget in 70 years, in contravention of the country's pacifist constitution, $42 billion. Tokyo's increased military expenditure comes amid rising tensions between Japan and China.

Below is a list of the world's largest arms manufacturers and other military service companies who profit the most from War Economies with their origin also shown. The information is based on a list published by the Stockholm International Peace Research Institute for 2013. The list provided by the SIPRI excludes companies based in China.

Rank	Company	Country	Arms sales ($US m.)	Total sales ($US m.)	Arms sales as a % of total sales	Total profit	Total employment
1	Lockheed Martin	United States	35 490	45 500	78	2 981	115000
2	Boeing	United States	30 700	86 623	35	4 585	168400
3	BAE Systems	United Kingdom	26 820	28 406	94	275	84600
4	Raytheon	United States	21 950	23 706	93	2 013	63000
5	Northrop Grumman	United States	20 200	24 661	82	1 952	65300
6	General Dynamics	United States	18 660	31 218	60	2 357	96000
7	EADS	European Union	15 740	78 693	20	1 959	144060
8	United Technologies Corporation	United States	11 900	62 626	19	5 721	212000
9	Finmeccanica	Italy	10 560	21 292	50	98	63840
10	Thales Group	France	10 370	18 850	55	761	65190

Institutes participating in weapon research and warfare simulation:

- Netherlands Organisation for Applied Scientific Research
- Bolt, Beranek and Newman
- QinetiQ
- Defense Advanced Research Projects Agency

Oscar Arias Sanchez, President of Costa Rica (awarded the Nobel Peace Prize in 1987 for his efforts to end civil wars across Central America through the Esquipulas II Accord) has stated:

"When a country decides to invest in arms, rather than in education, housing, the environment, and health services for its people, it is depriving a whole generation of its right to prosperity and happiness. We have produced one firearm for every ten inhabitants of this planet, and yet we have not bothered to end hunger when such a feat is well within our reach. Our international regulations allow almost three-quarters of all global arms sales to pour into the developing world with no binding international guidelines whatsoever. Our regulations do not hold countries accountable for what is done with the weapons they sell, even when the probable use of such weapons is obvious."

And now, June 2016, we have in excess of 60 million refugees around the world. Starvation and deprivation still plague the continents of Africa, Asia, Central and South America!

A sad indictment of my current home country (Australia) is that it spends a disproportionate amount of money on armaments and (from the author's point of view) has attended an excessive number of wars in recent decades. We are a big country with a big coastline but a small population. Our exports of oil, gas and minerals permit us to afford such extravagance... but at what cost to future generations? In 2014 we were ranked 8th among the greatest importers of military hardware! (But still have 50 000+ homeless living on the streets!)

Statement of the European Council to the United Nations General Assembly:

"We are committed to upholding, implementing and further

strengthening the multilateral disarmament and non-proliferation framework in the fight against threats which are tending to escape the control of national sovereignty, the challenges deriving from destabilising accumulation and spread of small arms and light weapons, from illicit or irresponsible arms trade, and from the proliferation of weapons of mass destruction, which are creating new and growing hot-spots of international tension. In this regard, the EU welcomes the growing support in all parts of the world for an International Arms Trade Treaty and is firmly committed to this process."

A noble gesture but with more than a hint of hypocrisy when consideration is taken regarding the production and sales of weapons! Even the US president, whilst trying to introduce more gun control has no power, so it seems, over weapons manufacture and export dollars earned from these! The inherent structure of the United Nations is also seen as problematic by the author, where the members of the inner clique are also the greatest manufacturers of armaments!

China's Slice of the Cake: China's global arms push continues. China showcased some of its military hardware to potential buyers in the Persian Gulf at the Dubai Air Show. The jewel in China's crown at the Air Show was the FC-31 stealth fighter (basically a replica of the F-35 Joint Strike Fighter–supposedly constructed with designs stolen from Lockheed-Martin back in 2009). Another interesting piece of news from Dubai was that China and Pakistan apparently have found an unnamed buyer for their jointly developed JF-17 "Thunder" fighter. China has had teams of aero-engineers building military aircraft in Pakistan for almost a decade now.

67

China had several other interesting items on show in Dubai. *Shaanxi Aircraft Corporation* has been promoting its venerable Y-8C and its modern Y-9 (basically the People's Liberation Army Air Force's version of a C-130 Hercules). According to the Moscow Centre for Analysis of Strategies and Technology, Iran has already ordered an undisclosed number of these aircraft. (Iran has already been seen to have airlifted troops to battlefields in Syria and has a requirement for more heavy transport aircraft.)

The bulk of China's armaments sales are to countries in the Middle East and Africa as well as nearer neighbours such as Pakistan. Current estimates of total arms sales (2015) are between $US5 billion and $US10 billion annually and rising. This pales into insignificance when compared to the procurements domestically to the People's National Liberation Armed Forces! Estimates here are around the $US40 billion mark annually! (this include $US3 billion imports from other countries.)

Interesting to note here how many Chinese 'copies' of US hardware have appeared in recent years. Many were acquired through cyber attacks and other methods, with the regime successfully having stolen large amounts of sensitive information, including military weapon blueprints from major corporations and government bureaus. Although the Chinese military regularly boasts about their so-called cutting-edge new technology, they still lag behind in weapons development. In 2011, Dongfan "Greg" Chung, an aerospace engineer from Orange County, was sentenced to 24 years and 5 months in prison for spying for the Chinese regime having stolen more than 250,000 documents from Boeing and Rockwell all posted home to mother China! Also, in July of 2014, a Chinese businessman was arrested for stealing data from the US regarding two dozen defence programs, including the F-35 and F-22.

Chinese copies include:

- Xi'an Aircraft Industrial Corporation built the Y-20, a heavy freighter aircraft closely resembling the C-17
- In late July of 2014, China's Chengdu Aircraft Corporation conducted a successful test flight of the Chengdu J-20, an aircraft combining designs and technology from the F-22 Raptor and F-35 Strike Fighter planes.
- Constructed by state-owned aircraft manufacturer China Academy of Aerospace Aerodynamics of the China Aerospace Science and Technology Corporation (CASC), the Cai Hong-4 (CH-4), or Rainbow-4 drone, is a multipurpose drone copying the US's MQ-1 Predator.
- In 2014, the regime revealed their new HJ-12 anti-tank missile able to target tanks over 2 miles away, Manufactured by China's state-owned company NORINCO (which has also been selling weapons to South Sudan) and is strikingly similar to the US's FGM-148 Javelin anti-tank missile in size, targeting systems, method of firing, and even basic design.
- In late 2013, China conducted a flight test of a Z-10 helicopter, which closely resembles the US's Sikorsky UH-60, popularly known as the "Black Hawk."
- After seeing the Humvee's abilities to cross deserts during the Gulf War in 1991, the Chinese military gained interest in the vehicle and gathered the few civilian Humvees that Chinese oil companies had bought in the 1990s as well as one AM General

had left on the mainland. Using reverse engineering they built a prototype and named it Dongfeng EQ2050.

Dongfeng EQ2050 (Boris van Hoytema)

- More recently the Chinese regime showed off its new microwave crowd-control weapon at a military technology exhibition. Mounted on a truck, the WB-1 millimeter-wave beam constructed by the China Poly Group Corporation fires non lethal beams on microwave frequency, heating up the water molecules just beneath the skin and making people feel a painful, burning sensation. The WB-1 has a range of 80 meters and can be enhanced to reach 1 kilometre. Used as a riot-control weapon by police makes it dangerous for civilian protesters or dissidents in China. This hideous weapon replicates the function and purpose of the Active Denial System (ADS), designed by the American defence contractor Raytheon. The ADS was actually deployed in Afghanistan in 2010 but never used!

WB-1 Weapon for crowd Control, China.

India is also a worrying exporter of military hardware with a massive explosion of overseas sales and accelerated growth in production. The major destinations for defence exports from India include Afghanistan, Algeria, Belgium, Ecuador, Indonesia, Israel, Myanmar, Nepal, Oman, Romania, Russia, South Korea, Sudan, Vietnam and the UK.

Among the major items being exported are offshore patrol vessels, spares for radars, Cheetal helicopters, turbo chargers and batteries, electronic systems, light engineering mechanical parts and personal protective items, which comprise articles like helmets, bulletproof jackets and other types of clothing. Government initiatives to encourage new industries in the armaments arena will push the country into ever more sophisticated hardware for world markets. Within a decade it is likely to fall a close second behind China with the United States falling to third place. As an importer of military hardware, India ranked at number one in 2014-2015 accounting for 14% of global trade rapidly expanding its budget to around $US10 billion!

71

For the peoples of the world we see a dark landscape looming where Governments and their short-lived politicians become ever more influenced by the ugly face of nationalism and the forces of greed and unchecked capitalism. War will become common place as the international conglomerates vie for sales of their deadly potions and explosives to foolish nations. Humans will suffer horrific injustices and murder by the warlords and their bursting warehouses of cruel machines and torture equipment to be unleashed like never before. The United Nations will become sterile and impotent as it is manipulated by these inhumane giants. The poor will remain impoverished with little hope of advancement or escape from their situation as huge percentages of economies of sovereign nations are poured down the drain of national pride and arrogance, seeping the very lifeblood of what might be defined as civilization! Deprivation, despair, excessive pain and destruction darken the horizons of what was once a beautiful planet full of hope and creativity.

Does it have to all end like this? Are these the scenarios that the average person wishes to experience? The momentum of population growth and inherent stagnation of environments through climate escalation and pollution are pressing problems enough without this extreme waste on unnecessary things such as armaments! The nations of the world are running headlong to helter-skelter without pausing to think of the consequences of both action and inaction. Inaction against madness and action down the wrong pathways! Empire building will not bring happiness and civilization to its highest potential. Respect and sensitivity to other cultures with a mind frame of working together, especially to avoid conflict, is the only safe way forward. A love of the environment and correct and intelligent action to maintain its delicate balance is now our only hope and saviour for a new world clean and safe for all. The day of the 'rod-of-iron' is over! The alternative is devastation and an end to the world as we have known it!

Only people at the grass roots level can dissolve the international war lords and conglomerates that continue to produce and stockpile weapons and military hardware. Individual nations have little or no power (and often no willpower) to prevent or stand up to this madness. The United Nations is also powerless against super capital ventures. Anyone seen to get in the way may conveniently be paid off or alternatively, disappear. The whole armament business globally is the greatest con and a prime factor in maintaining poverty. It is to my mind an expression of poverty in intellectualism and more akin to the urges of primitive man. Our media play an essential part in the whole international conspiracy of war games and war reality by keeping the public on edge and frightened. The bogey man under the bed sells newspapers and magazines as well as holding our attention on the TV screen.

International arms markets make me sick to the stomach. Yet many countries rely on the sale of weapons and military hardware as an essential portion of their economies. Armaments manufacturing secures jobs for millions around the world. But the fields and plains of war scenarios are scattered with the rotting limbs of men, women and children blown apart by bombs, missiles, landmines and shells. I say that politics has become manipulated by the evil of the war lords... i.e the company directors, share holders and the members of those work forces telling themselves (deceptively) that they are "serving their country" by working in an armaments factory. The rhetoric of totalitarian regimes and the rhetoric of the so called 'free western nations' is all the same! And the results and consequences are always the same!

As you can see I am already booked in for the Defence and Security Exhibition in London in Sep. 2017. I will be trying to sell my new 'Alpha-Omega Bomb' to would be purchasers for a very large sum: £1000 000 000 000 i.e one thousand billion British pounds sterling! I would imagine King John-un of North Korea might be interested but I don't think he can afford one just now! If detonated it would form a small black hole which would suck in the whole planet in the space of about three minutes. After a few hours it would suck in the sun and several of the inner planets. After a couple of years it will suck in Alpha Centauri and a few neighbouring stars. Actually I have only one completed just now, sitting in an abandoned mine under a hill... but then again, how many would one need?

The Russian Defence Ministry regularly carries out its massive expositions which display small arms and military hardware, drones, robotic systems, biotechnology, laser and radio technologies, military and medical facilities and new types of fuels on a 5,000-hectare display area outside Moscow. State arms distributor Rosoboronexport says it expects arms sales to foreign buyers to remain steady over coming years with total sales close to the $15 billion mark exporting to around 60 countries worldwide. Russia remains the world's second biggest seller of arms behind the United States.

[Incidentally, Russian intelligence officer, Aleksandr Poteyev, who was sentenced for treason in absentia by Russia after blowing the cover of a spy ring in the US, has reportedly died … July 2016]

Military Fairs and Expos for 2016-2017:

"Roll up, roll up, get your best fireworks here… all guaranteed to blow off arms, heads and legs of women and children at any time and at any place in the world… roll up, roll up… get your bargain weapons here from only reputable companies and manufacturers with a long history of perfection, expertise and precision… roll up, roll up, roll up!"

Whatever happened to the peace movements of the 1960s and 1970s? They grew old and their songs and poetry forgotten? Where is the new generation of protestors? I am certain the invigorating energy of intelligent youth still has its mark to make for peace in the world!

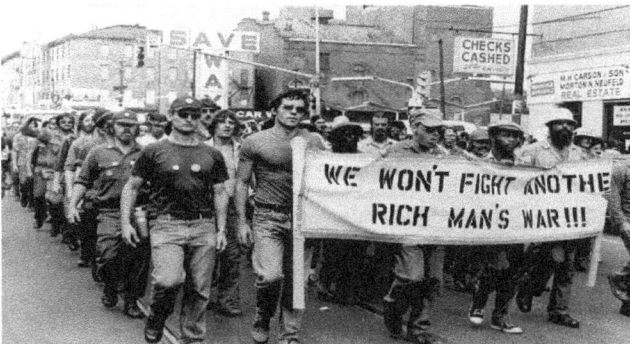

Are You a Private Private?

It has been said that more deaths have occurred in Afghanistan to Private Security personnel than deaths of American servicemen. The growth of the private security industry in the US, the UK, Australia and other countries has blossomed into a multibillion dollar enterprise. But it is a worry and there are serious questions to be asked. The most prominent of course are these:

'is there any relation between private security companies and arms and armament manufacturers?'

'are private security companies usurping the roles of national police forces and the armed forces?'

'is there a danger of private security companies morphing into private armies?'

These possible relationships are highly dangerous to our democracies and even to our elected governments and their jurisdictions. I am not a professor of law, but one doesn't need such a qualification to understand the simple principle of evolution:

- ➜ Humankind invents government
- ➜ Government creates and controls armies and police forces
- ➜ Government hires private armies (and robots)
- ➜ Private armies (and robots) take over from Government
- ➜ Private controllers control everything!

The Australian Government cannot help itself. As stated before, it tends to follow overseas trends generally as 'sane and good ideas!' But it has not always been proven to be the case. The arguments for 'privatisation' of public utilities has always been 'they can do the job better and cheaper'. But our overseas gulags for refugees (you know, some of those poor 60+ million souls displaced by war and totalitarian regimes at the hands of wicked people smugglers that might be described as tourists without visas) have cost tax payers exorbitant sums. But our conservative politicians only learned a single nursery rhyme as small children: "privatise, privatise, privatise, privatise…" Their first xmas present is usually a very large wooden mallet which has printed on its side in large red letters "UNION BASHER!"

The following is a list of some of the more prominent companies that assist governments and armed forces worldwide, providing highly trained armed personnel and logistical support:

ACADEMI:

Originally going under the name Blackwater USA, American private military company ACADEMI was established in 1997 by ex-US Navy SEAL Erik Prince. Blackwater was awarded its first government contract in 2000, and in order for the company to fulfill it, more than 100,000 sailors were trained for action. Blackwater was heavily – and controversially – involved in the Iraq War. It works with "federal, state and local government clients, global commercial customers, numerous law enforcement and intelligence organizations and agencies and allied governments worldwide."

ICTS International:

Former Israel Security Agency and El Al Israel Airlines security personnel formed Israeli private security company ICTS International N.V. in 1982. The firm's head office is in Amstelveen in the Netherlands. ICTS International provides advanced, comprehensive security solutions for the aviation and homeland security sectors, with an emphasis on transportation security in general, railroad and mass transport security in particular. ICTS International created a computer technology called Advanced Passenger Screening, which is utilized by the majority of US airlines. Based on passenger information, the algorithm calculates the likelihood of passengers posing some kind of threat. In 2008 ICTS International's revenue totalled $98.8 million.

Northbridge Services Group:

Registered in the Dominican Republic, but with offices in Kentucky, Ukraine and the UK, Northbridge Services Group is a private military contractor that claims to provide highly confidential and effective security related services designed to address the needs of governments, multinational corporations, non-governmental organizations, the corporate sector and prominent individuals. Northbridge's current CEO, Vietnam veteran Robert Kovacic, took up his post in 2003. The company's key services include security advisory and training, operational and intelligence support, and strategic communications. Northbridge also supports law enforcement agencies in the realm of terrorism, narcotics, organized crime, poaching, smuggling, maritime defense and the protection of natural resources. In 2012 Northbridge's revenue totaled $50.5 million.

Triple Canopy:

Triple Canopy is a private security, risk management and defence contracting company based in Reston, Virginia. Former US Special Forces soldiers established the firm in Chicago in 2003, and a significant number of Triple Canopy's employees are former special ops personnel and police officers. The company provides mission support, security and training services to government agencies and multinational corporations worldwide. Triple Canopy employs no less than 5,500 staff, and its clients include NGOs, telecommunication companies, oil and gas businesses, mining firms and financial organizations from all around the world. The company's chain of command counts former Delta Force soldiers, consultants and analysts among its number. Triple Canopy rose to prominence in 2004 in Iraq, and one of its Iraq defence contracts is valued at $1.5 billion.

Prosegur:

Prosegur is a multinational private security company with 150,000 staff spread out over Europe, Asia, Oceania and Latin America. The firm was established in 1976, and its head office is located in Madrid. Its service areas comprise manned guarding, home security, fire defence, and security technology and consulting. Prosegur is Spain's biggest private security firm; in 2011 the firm earned $233.748 million. With a task force of over 4,700 armoured vans, Prosegur is well known for its cash-in-transit services, which it outsources to banks around the world.

The company's technology services include CCTV monitoring, access control, and anti-intrusion and perimeter detection. Guarding provisions feature armed and unarmed guards as well as K-9 units and VIP protection.

Aegis Defence Services:

Aegis Defence Services is a British private military company established in 2002 by former Sandline International director and British soldier Tim Spicer. The firm has foreign offices in Iraq, Kenya, Nepal, Afghanistan, Bahrain and the USA. It also had a hand in the establishment of the British Association of Private Security Companies. The company is involved with NGO, aerospace, and government and diplomatic sectors, as well as oil, gas and mining industries. Currently, Aegis has a $293 million contract with the US government to provide protection and assistance during the restructuring of Iraq. In 2011 the company also secured a $497 million contract to protect the US Embassy situated in Kabul, Afghanistan.

GK Sierra:

Founded in 2007, Washington D.C. and Portland based private military company GK Sierra started out producing secure communication technology for the US government. Two years later, the firm, which is a wing of Genoa-Knowlton, Inc., started offering investigation and intelligence options among its services. At present

GK Sierra gathers intelligence for the CIA. As well as having a Tel-Aviv office, the company is said to employ high-ranking Mossad operatives, which has led to accusations that it is in fact part of the Israeli Intelligence Service – allegations that GK Sierra has emphatically rejected. The company's specialties include corporate investigation and intelligence, digital forensics, and encryption technology, while it is also purported to have direct action operatives on the ground in various countries around the world.

KBR:

KBR is a private military, engineering and construction company based in Houston. Formed in 1998, KBR has worked in countries like Cuba, Kosovo and Afghanistan. Currently, its American workforce in Iraq numbers 14,000, and it is also said to have the biggest US government contract there. In 2008, KBR declared that it was buying Alabama's BE&K in a deal said to be worth $550 million. In 2011 KBR earned $540 million. Today it employs more than 27,000 people in over 70 countries across Europe, the Americas, Africa, Asia, Australia and the Middle East. Over the years, the firm has, however, been involved in its share of controversies, from allegations of sexual assault lodged by female employees, to paying off Nigerian officials for government contracts.

Corps Security:

Formerly known as the Corps of Commissionaires, Corps Security is a British security company that reports to Queen Elizabeth II. Established in 1859, it is said to be the world's oldest security firm, and today it has a team of about 3,000 security personnel plus a dozen offices throughout the UK The company's specialty is corporate security and claims to be the leading supplier of specialist security solutions. Dressed in the company's iconic Commissionaire Uniforms, Corps Security's event protection unit secures high-profile sites like Wembley Stadium and the London Lord Mayor Show. Services include manned guarding, CCTV surveillance, alarm response and key holding.

Defion Internacional:

Headquartered in Lima, Peru, Defion Internacional is a private military company that supplies specialist security staff who are mostly recruited from Latin America. These personnel are often contracted out to other companies; in fact, Defion Internacional first became known when it trained recruits to work with Triple Canopy in Iraq. Defion Internacional has bureaus in Sri Lanka, the Philippines, Iraq and Dubai, and specializes in training bodyguards, drivers, logistics and administrative personnel. Latin American security staff stationed in the Middle East have been described as 'guns for hire.' A Peruvian in Baghdad will not panic if he has to face a blast or a blackout because he has already experienced that on the streets of Lima!

ICTS Europe:

Established as an independent company in 1999, ICTS Europe is a global expert in the provision of leading edge security solutions for the transportation and public safety industries. It offers rail, corporate and energy protection services, but its specialty is airport and airline security. ICTS Europe has K-9, technology and global solutions capabilities. The firm currently works with more than 250 rail, education, business, health, aviation and public sector groups in Africa,

Asia, the Middle East and Europe. Clients include Air France, Emirates, Etihad Airways, British Airways, and major airports like London's Gatwick and Heathrow. In 2012 it brought in more than $479 million in revenue.

Chubb Fire & Security:

English brothers Charles and Jeremiah Chubb established the company now known as Chubb Fire & Security in 1818, introducing its first safe in 1835. In the 1870s it expanded to the USA. At the time, the country was suffering from violent bank robberies, so Chubb responded by producing a time lock to be attached to the doors of vaults and safes. In 2000 Chubb sold its lock division and switched its focus to security systems. Since 2003 the firm has been owned by US multinational conglomerate United Technologies Corporation. In the UK, services include mobile patrols, remote surveillance and response, and key holding. Meanwhile, South African extras comprise armed response teams, electric fencing, and a special Chubb911 24-hour emergency hotline. In Australia, the company also offers a cash-in-transit service.

Andrews International:

Established in Los Angeles in 1988, Andrews International is a California-based private security firm with offices across America. It boasts branches in Mexico, Honduras and Colombia and has operatives in Canada and India. Andrews International provides armed and unarmed security guards for businesses as well as offering specialist government and defence department solutions. In 2009 it bought Canadian global security giant GardaWorld's US and Mexican guarding services for a sum exceeding $44 million. Andrews

International security personnel protect national landmarks, major tourist attractions, industrial sites, educational and financial institutions, healthcare facilities, and other locations where security stakes and client expectations are high.

Asia Security Group:

Asia Security Group is a somewhat mysterious Afghanistan based private security company that offers a range of consultancy and manpower support services to government and corporate clients to improve capability and ensure security. The company has branches in Kabul, Mazar-e-Sharif, Jalalabad and Kandahar and boasts a team of licensed armed troops, promising comprehensive security solutions while mitigating risks across Afghanistan. Asia Security Group has worked with US forces in Afghanistan, guarding supply convoys in war-torn parts of the country. The company's personnel have also joined up with the US private military firm DynCorp. Services include security, risk assessment and management, and business development.

Erinys International:

British private security firm Erinys International has a head office in Cyprus as well as branches in the UK, South Africa, and the Republic and Democratic Republic of Congo. The company operates within the mineral extraction, oil and gas, public, and NGO markets, and boasts an infrastructural development division. In each of these areas, it helps clients to appreciate risks they may face even in remote and challenging the environments. Erinys International was launched in 2001 by former British soldier Jonathan Garratt. Erinys South Africa was added in 2002, and the company has had a presence in a number of locations in Africa and the Middle East. In 2003 the firm worked with the Iraq Ministry of Oil, training and supplying a 16,000-strong Oil Protection Force guarding 282 sites.

TSU Protection Services:

Former South African policeman and Special Forces officer Chris Beukes founded TSU Protection Services in 1999, and now claims to be one of South Africa's top private security firms. "As a police officer the pay was adequate but not great, so I decided to launch TSU Protection Services to meet the gap in the market." Now, with a force of highly trained operatives, the company serves high-profile businesses and other clients. Its specialties include armed personal escorts, executive protection and support, crowd control, and maritime security.

International Intelligence Limited:

International Intelligence Limited is a British firm that focuses on counter-espionage and investigations. It was formed in 2002 by ex-aide to the British Royal Family Alex Bomberg. The company offers private investigation, technical surveillance counter-measure, intelligence, counter-intelligence, counter-surveillance and counter-espionage services. Employees comprise former law enforcement, military, financial investigation and intelligence personnel. Specialist services include financial forensics, computer forensic analysis and satellite tracking. International Intelligence Limited has operated in the private, corporate and commercial sectors, as well as with government agencies, embassies and police forces.

Unity Resources Group:

Australian firm Unity Resources Group was founded in 2000, and although its personnel are largely Antipodean, the company's head office is in Dubai, UAE. Unity Resources Group offers crisis, risk, security, logistics, aviation, executive and medical services. It is a solutions provider of land, sea and air services in complex, challenging and fragile environments where dependable infrastructure may not be present. The firm has offices in Europe, Australasia, Africa, North and South America, the Middle East and Central Asia employing more than 1,200 people. Unity Resources Group provides event security, security in high-risk zones, asset security and guarding. In 2007 some of its operatives were involved in a controversial incident in Baghdad in which two civilians were killed. The firm defended the conduct of its employees… naturally!

Senaca Group:

The Senaca Group is a wide-ranging private security firm based in Ireland. The company includes Senaca EU and Senaca Canada and conducts operations around the world. Subdivisions comprise Senaca Guarding, Senaca Cash Management Services, Senaca Training, Senaca Tech, and private security company Integrated Risk Management Services. The firm works within the oil and gas, transport and logistics, financial, tourism, government, health, property, maritime, energy, NGO, and policing sectors. Integrated Risk Management Services offers guards, patrols, corporate security, alarm response and key holding. Senaca Cash Management Services specializes in the transportation of money. At the same time, Senaca Tech affords a range of surveillance and access control solutions technology. Ex-Irish Army Special Forces major Jim Farrell and security veteran Terry Downes co-founded the Senaca Group in 2009. They also co-founded Integrated Risk Management Services in 2005.

Pinkerton Government Services:

Spy and detective Allan Pinkerton founded the Pinkerton National Detective Agency in Chicago in 1850. Nowadays, Pinkerton Government Services offers a full range of cleared protective services designed to meet the specific requirements of the US government. It provides regular security services such as guards, fire fighting and emergency medical technicians, as well as specialized resources like sniffer dogs. In 2003 Pinkerton was acquired by Swedish security giant Securitas AB, and switched its name to Securitas Critical Infrastructure.

The Brink's Company:

Based in Virginia, The Brink's Company has a network that dots the global landscape operating in over 100 countries with a staff of roughly 70,000. Perry Brink established Brink's City Express in Chicago in 1859. Brink's is perhaps best known for its fleet of armoured vans, which it uses to help see to the needs of governments, mints, banks, jewellers and other businesses. It also offers ICD and airport security, guarding, and logistical and cash management services. In 2011 Brink's brought in $3.9 billion in revenue.

CACI International:

CACI International was founded in Santa Monica, California in 1962, the acronym signifying the Consolidated Analysis

89

Center Incorporated. CACI International has more than 120 branches and employs around 15,000 people throughout the US and Europe. The firm's area of expertise is information technology, and it provides information solutions and services in support of national security missions and government transformation for intelligence, defence, and federal civilian customers. CACI International plays a role in assisting with matters concerning global threats and the readiness of America's armed forces. In 2012 the company's revenue was $3.8 billion.

Booz Allen Hamilton:

US tech consulting company Booz Allen Hamilton has head offices in Tysons Corner, Virginia, founded in 1914. In 2012 and its revenue reached almost $6 billion. Booz Allen Hamilton's areas of service include engineering, management consulting and technology, but it also operates as a defence contractor. The company works with civilian and government institutions providing consulting and professional services in an increasingly complex and growing world. As far as civilian agencies go, the firm serves the financial, policing, transport, Homeland Security, and government health and management sectors. It also works with the US Army, Air Force, Navy and Marine Corps, as well as defence organizations, space agencies and intelligence groups.

Control Risks:

Based in London, England with 36 offices around the world, Control Risks is an international professional services and consulting firm dedicated to helping organizations manage political, integrity and security risks in complex and hostile environments. Control Risks began as a division of insurance firm Hogg Robinson in 1975 and then became independent in 1982. As major companies around the world began working in lesser-known areas in the 1990s, Control Risks focused on developing its intelligence and investigation services. It provides strategic consultancy, expert analysis and in-depth investigations through to handling sensitive political issues and providing practical on-the-ground protection and support. Following its work in Iraq securing oil company assets, Control Risks generated $223 million in revenue in 2010.

GardaWorld:

Canadian firm GardaWorld claims to be the largest privately-owned security company in the world. The company's headquarters are in Montreal, Quebec, but it employs around 45,000 people across North America, Europe, Africa, Asia, Latin America and the Middle East. GardaWorld secures individuals and resources in at least 140 cities and protects 28 North American airports. Its international protective services department aims to safeguard clients in complex and emerging markets. The company's cash management services process $5 billion a day. In August 2013 GardaWorld acquired G4S' Canadian cash management division in a deal thought to be worth around $110 million. In December 2013 GardaWorld agreed upon a 12-year cash management deal with Bank of America valued at $1.4 billion. At the end of April 2012, GardaWorld's quarterly revenue totalled some $300 million.

DynCorp:

Virginia-based private military contractor DynCorp stretches back to 1951, when Land-Air, Inc. was obtained by California Eastern Airways to form what would become California Eastern Aviation, Inc. In 1962 the company was renamed Dynalectron Corporation, which was renamed DynCorp in 1987.

DynCorp's services include security, aviation support, intelligence, and contingency ops. The firm's yearly revenue exceeds $3 billion, and over 96 percent of that figure is generated by US government contracts. DynCorp has provided support for the US forces in countries like Peru, Colombia, Somalia, Kosovo, Kuwait, Bolivia, Angola and Haiti.

AlliedBarton:

AlliedBarton is a Pennsylvania-based private security company that was established in 1957. Staffed by over 55,000 employees divided among 120 offices around the USA, AlliedBarton is the biggest US owned security officer business in America. The company focuses on various different areas, including higher education campuses, commercial property, aerospace and defence sites, housing, malls, healthcare facilities, and chemical industries. Through its 'Hire Our Heroes' program, AlliedBarton recruits former members of the armed forces, reservists and their relatives to bolster its staff of highly trained security personnel. In November 2013 Victory Media included AlliedBarton on its 2014 lists of Top Military Friendly and Military Spouse Friendly companies to work for. The firm specializes in local response and national support. In 2012 its annual revenue exceeded $1.9 billion.

ADT:

ADT Corporation was founded in 1874 and today is one of America's leading alarm and security monitoring companies. Based in Boca Ranton, Florida, the company operates in 35 countries around the world, supplying alarms, monitoring equipment and peace of mind to homes and small businesses. In South Africa, ADT provides armed response teams and around-the-clock surveillance. In 2011 ADT boasted an estimated 6.4 million clients and yearly turnover of $3.1 billion.

Securitas AB:

Established in Helsingborg, Sweden in 1934, Securitas AB is a worldwide security company with head offices in Stockholm. In 2012 the company had around 300,000 workers spread out over 53 countries and annual revenue of over $10 billion. Securitas AB's services include guards and patrols, investigations, home alarm systems, loss prevention, security consulting and guard dog supply. Its three chief departments are Security Services Europe, Security Services Ibero-America and Security Services North America. To facilitate its cash in transit service, Securitas AB operates specialist vehicles with metal safes as well as a fleet of bulletproof jeeps. It also specializes in securing sporting, business and recreational events.

G4S:

G4S is possibly the world's leading global security and outsourcing group specializing in outsourcing of business processes in sectors where security and safety risks are considered a strategic threat. The British multinational security giant was set up in 2004 when London based company Securicor amalgamated with Danish business Group 4 Falck. Currently G4S employs more than 620,000 people, which makes it the third biggest employer in the private sector globally. In 2012 G4S turned over more than $12 billion. The company offers a range of services, including the supply of security personnel, monitoring equipment, response units and secure prisoner transportation. G4S also works with governments overseas to deliver security.

It is assumed that all these firms are an essential part in maintaining 'world safety' from all the bad guys. Tom Law wonders whether they are also symptomatic of 'world problems' specifically in the spread of armaments, terrorism and petite wars! Why do I say this? Because capitalism must vent its spleen to make a profit and more money and wealth for the few. Many of these security firms work for government and national armed forces around the world as well as the Mr Giant mining companies and oil producing companies. With all the competition going on, it is in their interest that 'hot spot world problems' are ongoing... even if it means artificially creating and staging them. The problem for us ordinary folk is that these firms are often too closely associated with the armaments and gun manufacturing industries. Naturally they need to purchase their wares in order to operate. I am not in favour of these private companies involved in 'crowd control'. They always employ ex-police or ex-military combatants and many were founded by the same!

The most extreme view (held by some) of terrorist groups such as al Qaeda and ISIL and affiliates are that these organisations have been synthetically created and staged by very clever elements in the secretive world of 'intelligence'. Tom does not hold that view but proffers the hypothesis "it is not beyond the realm of possibility that

94

some organisations and consequential wars are artificially created to maintain the business of war and the necessity of private security firms and companies".

In my view, the bulk of national security is the job of government via its police forces, armed forces and intelligence organisations. *Private armies are a dangerous concept and equally pose a threat to democratic institutions and public safety as the criminals that they are supposedly protecting us from!*

Arguments put forward by DFAT (Dept. of Foreign Affairs and Trade) in Australia for tendering Private Security:

DFAT argues that it is more efficient and effective to use private security in both locations (Iraq and Afghanistan) because contractors can be mobilised more quickly than the military and often have "high quality and contemporary skill-sets, invaluable in-country knowledge, and experience in specific operating environments". Many of the Australian contractors at the Baghdad and Kabul embassies are highly trained ex–special forces personnel with previous multiple tours in both countries. Both civilian and military officials privately acknowledge that one of the main reasons security at the Baghdad embassy was outsourced was because the ADF was running low on military police with skills in close personal protection. In both cases, too, private security companies travelling in unmarked four-wheel drives offer a lower profile than uniformed military personnel travelling in convoys of green armoured vehicles. And often DFAT prefers the direct control of managing a contract with a private company, rather than the constant negotiations and friction that can come when diplomatic protocols intersect with military culture.

There is another reason – an unspoken one – why DFAT prefers to use private security personnel in Iraq and Afghanistan, and that's the lower political risk of deploying civilian security professionals. There has been little parliamentary or public interest in Australia's private armies in Baghdad and Kabul, and when a contractor is killed or injured there is no ramp ceremony or grand political funeral that accompanies the arrival of their body back onto Australian soil!

I don't find any of these arguments convincing. Again, it is purely another example of modern era governments shirking responsibility but at an unacceptable financial cost.

Further:

The main reason DFAT employs private security companies is to outsource much of the risk associated with running a large team prepared to use lethal force against a local attack. Security contractors are responsible for their own insurance and if a contractor is injured it is the company and not DFAT that bears the responsibility of providing medical aid, evacuation and ongoing rehabilitation.

Excerpts from article by James Brown for The Monthly

https://www.themonthly.com.au/issue/2014/may/1398866400/james-brown/guns-hire

In other words, *Australians working for Private Security Firms are expendable and not worth worrying about!* The other unpalatable element is that there is already a self-fulfilling cycle of Government military personnel becoming soldiers of fortune in these private armies.

China enters the Private Security market:

> Over 35,000 Chinese citizens needed to be evacuated when unrest took place in Libya in 2011. The following year, armed Chinese security contractors, in conjunction with local military forces, helped rescue 29 kidnapped Chinese workers in the Sudan. There are commercial and reputational reasons for Chinese companies operating overseas to employ Chinese PSCs. Chinese private security firms have been encouraged in their overseas activities by the Chinese Government, particularly through national government legislation and privatisation efforts. At the same time that Chinese PSCs are being driven to expand overseas, non-Chinese PSCs have been establishing their presence within China. G4S, for example, established a Chinese subsidiary in 2001 that now employs over 1,500 staff to provide technical security services, guarding and risk consultancy.
>
> Most Chinese PSCs provide low-end guarding services for Chinese-owned business and close personal protection services for Chinese workers. China City Guard, for example, has been providing security for Chinese state-owned enterprise property (particularly mining sites) since 2005. In South Africa, Sino South African Security and Zhonghua Xuanlong security

provide armed guards for Chinese Privateers in Australia's Conflict and Disaster Zones, markets, restaurants and factories. Many of these Chinese companies working in Africa subcontracted guard work to local national personnel, most of whom do not have military experience. In some of the more dangerous African countries (Nigeria, Rwanda, DRC and the Congo) bad experiences with locally engaged security personnel led to a resurgence in employment of Chinese nationals in security roles.

- Extract from paper by Australian Government - Australian Civilian-Military Centre, "Privateers in Australia's Conflict and Disaster Zones" 1/2015 James Brown, ACMC Consultant.

With the advent of digital networks, there will soon be little or no need for armoured security vans to transport vast quantities of cash.

The vigilante or mercenary mind-set will also be out-dated with stronger law enforcement. However there will always remain some people that wish to join with private forces based on their innate desire "to kill" but in a protected or legal way. Personally I would like to see the majority of private security firms disenfranchised and shut down for their dirty business forever! Yes, perhaps Tom Law has now made more enemies in the world... and powerful ones too! Amen!

Death in America

May 08, 2016 Mothers, Celebrities Rally Against Gun Violence

On Mother's Day weekend, hundreds of people marched across the Brooklyn Bridge to demand stricter gun laws. This Saturday was the fourth annual march with mothers providing anecdotes to the media on the gun deaths of their children in recent years. Placards called for America to turn to common sense regarding current attitudes to gun laws held by society, with strong appeals for radical change!

With so many guns in America it comes as no surprise that there are so many gun related deaths. These fall into the categories:

- Accidental shootings
- Murders or homicides (includes domestic violence, contract killings)
- Mass killings
- Shootings by the police and related services
- Shootings by Private Security Services

It is far more probable that one might be shot by either a sibling or by a member of the police force than by a terrorist!

A man shot in Oakland California became the 1,000th database entry in *'The Counted'*, an ongoing investigation by the Guardian to record every fatality caused by police and other law enforcement officers in 2015, to monitor the demographics of the people who died and detail how and why they were killed. This was the 883rd fatal shooting by a law enforcement officer so far in 2015, according to the Guardian's records. Another 47 people died after being shocked with an officer's Taser, 33 died after being struck by a law enforcement officer's vehicle, and 36 were killed in custody. Another received a deadly blow to the head during a fight with an officer.

The shooting was also the 183rd death recorded in California, by far the greatest total of any state. Nine states, however, have recorded more deaths per capita, with Oklahoma having the highest rate.

An FBI director said earlier that it was 'ridiculous and embarrassing' that the Guardian and a separate project by the Washington Post had better information than the Federal Government about deaths at the hands of law enforcement officers. The US government publishes no comprehensive record of people killed by law enforcement, even after a series of controversial deaths unleashed a national protest movement and demands from activists and lawmakers alike for better data on the subject.

The Counted was launched on 1 June 2015, logging 464 deaths in the year to that point. At that time 102 or 22% of those killed had been unarmed. This proportion has since fallen slightly to 20% or 198 of the total 1,000. In 59 deaths, however, it remains unclear whether the suspect was armed.

As of 1 June, black Americans were more than twice as likely to be unarmed as white Americans when killed by police. Up until June 1st, 32% of the 135 black people killed by police had been unarmed, compared with 15% of the 234 white people. This disparity has since shrunk, with 26% of the 248 black people and 18% of 490 white people being recorded as unarmed. On average, an unarmed black man was fatally shot by police every nine days in the first seven months of 2015!

Brittany Packnett, a member of Barack Obama's taskforce on 21st century policing and a founder of the *Campaign Zero* movement that lobbies to curb the levels of police violence in America, said the milestone should be met with "sadness, but not deep shock".

"Black folks like me have known for a long time that the police do not always represent safety for us and that an encounter could be deadly," said Packnett. "But having these statistics that add to our personal stories should continue to move everyone towards wanting to play a part in correcting this."

Obama's taskforce, convened after unrest in Ferguson, followed the decision not to prosecute the white officer who shot dead Michael

Brown, an unarmed black 18-year-old, and made the collection of more reliable data on the number of police killings in the US one of its central recommendations. Further, Packnett said that while the government was still in the beginning stages of instigating the process, campaigners realised "it's not enough just to talk about police involved shootings... we have to talk about in-custody deaths, we have to talk about non-lethal police violence, we need to talk about particularly vulnerable communities like children."

The Washington Post's analysis showed that *black men were seven times more likely than white men to die by police gunfire while unarmed!*

18 law officers were shot and killed in the line of duty by a suspect this year (2015), including a Memphis police officer who died after a routine traffic stop. It has instilled fear that the legacy of Ferguson will include a higher death toll for police.

"Police are worried that officers who rely on their intuition and training to make a split-second decision - which could mean life or death for them - won't do it. The fear of being second-guessed, and perhaps even prosecuted, will take over instead" said the executive director of the national Fraternal Order of Police.

Death of Anthony Bartley, Yulee, Florida: "Several neighbors called the police on Anthony after he had gotten in a fight with someone whose house he spent the night at. One officer came, they got in an argument, the officer used a Taser gun on him but claims it did not have the desired effect. The officer then proceeded to shoot him once, when Anthony did not go to the

ground the officer shot him 4 or 5 more times until he was
pronounced dead.

He was 21 years old."

There is a plethora of similar anecdotal stories across the country- far
too many to cite here. Is this good enough for 21st century America? Is
this continued state of affairs what the majority of its citizens desire?
Does this behaviour by certain officers fall into the rational of
'Keeping America Safe'? Does it sit comfortably with the Constitution
and the Bill of Rights?

Any failure to comply indicates a threat!
A shot to the chest or head is the best line of defence!

It seems that each of these concepts is drilled into many of our men
and women in the police forces both in America and here in my own
country, Australia. Far too many cases of innocent behaviour or
misunderstood circumstances have resulted in the death of an innocent
person or a person committing some very minor misdemeanour. Even
an agitated minor waving a knife whilst facing three or more officers
does not deserve death by shooting. This is no less than an execution
and is both unacceptable and unjustified as well as being a mark of a
barbaric society! But hey, we don't just see police on our streets armed
with a hand gun... we now witness quasi military police armed with
fully automatic weapons and dressed with very sophisticated
protection. In fact many wear balaclavas and are sometimes
indistinguishable from terrorists! Perhaps in a real terrorist situation
there is a need for a specialist team. But we have been drugged by TV
and movies where this type of policing is common on the screen for
dubious cases where the villains are far less a threat than your terrorist.

Has the world become a more dangerous place because of terrorists alone or is there a new force controlling society in a sledge-hammer-over-the-top excessive way? Again and again we hear the same old catch cry from politicians and Police Commissioners "we are keeping you safe". Frankly I don't buy it!

Case of Keara Crowder

Memphis Tennessee: Keara was the officer's wife. The officer killed her and also shot, but did not kill her son in a domestic incident. The officer has since been charged with murder.

She was 29 years old.

This was a police officer killing his spouse!

Case of Dontre Hamilton

Milwaukee Wisconsin: Hamilton, an unarmed mentally ill man, was lying on the ground near Red Arrow Park when a police officer ordered him to move, then proceeded to pat him down. The officer tried to hit Hamilton with a baton, which Hamilton allegedly took away and attempted to hit the officer with it. The officer shot Hamilton 14 times, including in the back. Hamilton died at the scene.

He was 31 years old.

I seem to have read of so many incidences where the shootings did not involve say one, two or three bullets, more like this example of fourteen and as many as seventeen shots to the one person. The desired outcome is definitely death. But why so many bullets? Why not just go to a shooting range if the said officer wishes to blow off steam or just fire away willy nilly?

The case of Iretha Lilly

Waco, Texas: Iretha died after being shocked with an electric stun gun while deputies tried to take her into custody.

She was 37 years old.

What can I say? The world knows the sort of things that go on in Waco!

I have seen this ad in Oz also… personally I find it pathetic, laughable but somewhat scary at the same time. It clearly demonstrates the advocating, propagating, substantiating and continual support of *"the culture of fear"* inherent in 21st century America. But the bottom line is: it's another adjunct to the great imperial capitalistic trend of making profit out of the psychological misery of the masses by forever instilling fear and insecurity!

> *"In times like these, it's more important than ever for Americans to be prepared for anything, and this flashlight is one of the best pieces of gear to have as it can be used in almost every situation, from self defense to finding your dog at night…"*

I see an explosion of 'blind dogs' lost in the suburbs any day soon!

In the Australian version the ad says:

> Just released to the public, a new and powerful tactical military flashlight called the LightStrike 360 ™ utilizes military-grade technology that was previously used by elite US NAVY Seals… and further: the "strobe mode" can temporarily disorient and blind a threat without having to use deadly force.

In other words it can be used as a mild weapon. One hopes that the government department 'Australian Standards' might see this and take it off the market. However it is hard to stop imports of such devices (including lasers and masers) by private customers that purchase via the internet!

5 Modes
High
Medium
Low
SOS
Strobe

Telescoping Focus
X 1
X 250
X 500
X 1000
X 2000

T6-2000

Aircraft Grade
Aluminum

Ultra Light &
Ultra Tough

100,000 Hours
Lamp Life

Beveled Edge
For Self Defense

Cree XM-L T6 Bulb

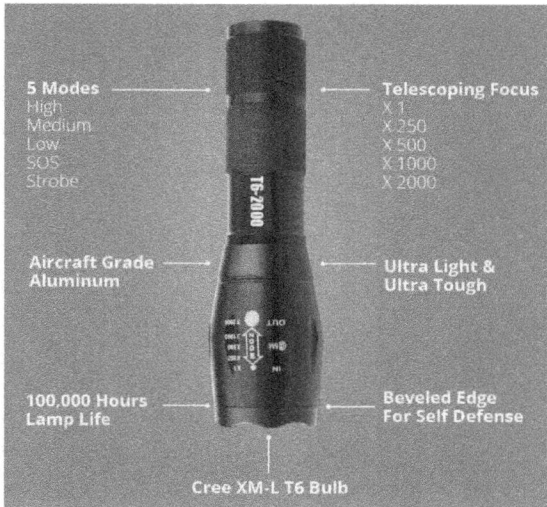

Shoot First, Question Later:

"Sir, please step out your car". They say it twice, he doesn't get out of the car. Then they open fire.

No matter what the excuse, unless it is clear that someone is armed and threatening, an officer of the law should never draw his/her weapon and shoot a citizen. This is murder. This is an execution. This is unconscionable and unforgivable. This, in fact, is the perpetration of a crime!

Between August 9th 2014 and August 8th 2015 it was reported that at least 1,083 Americans were killed by police across America according to comprehensive research and data collected by VICE News. This calculates to an average of nearly three people a day!

California	176	Tennessee	27	N Carolina	19	Iowa	4
Florida	80	Washington	22	Oregon	18	Maine	5
Texas	110	Alabama	20	Pennsylv.	21	Montana	4
Arizona	48	Indiana	17	S Carolina	19	Nebraska	8
Colorado	22	Kansas	16	Utah	14	N Hamps.	2
Georgia	33	Kentucky	19	Virginia	16	Nth Dakota	1
Illinois	25	Maryland	17	Alaska	2	Rhode Isl	0
Louisiana	24	Massachus.	12	Arkansas	6	Sth Dakota	2
Missouri	23	Michigan	16	Connecticut	3	Vermont	0
New Jersey	25	Minnesota	13	DC	3	W Virginia	8
New York	31	Mississippi	13	Delaware	4	Wisconsin	1 0
Ohio	34	Nevada	14	Hawaii	6	Wyoming	4
Oklahoma	32	New Mex.	15	Ohio	6		

Table: Number of people killed in US by police Aug 2014 – Aug 2015

While the majority of those killed from August 2014 to August 2015 were white, black people were more than twice as likely to be killed by cops than any other race. Afro-Americans are more than three times as likely to be killed by police than white people, according to these statistics. Brown's death was a seminal moment in arousing US consciousness of structural racial bias in police departments around the country, and the grand jury's decision three months later not to indict the Ferguson police officer who killed him, proved to many that that bias permeates every facet of the criminal justice system.

Now, in July 2016, America is at a pivotal point!

In the words of President Barack Obama, acknowledged at a press conference immediately after the Ferguson grand jury decision in November:

"In too many parts of this country a deep distrust exists between law enforcement and communities of color. Some of this is the result of the legacy of racial discrimination in this country."

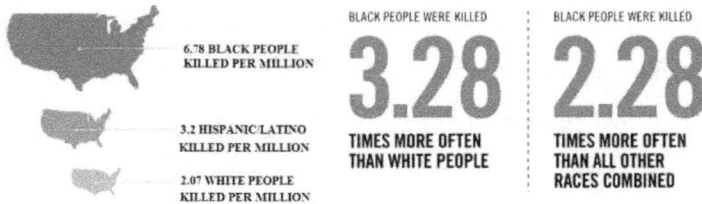

6.78 BLACK PEOPLE KILLED PER MILLION

3.2 HISPANIC/LATINO KILLED PER MILLION

2.07 WHITE PEOPLE KILLED PER MILLION

BLACK PEOPLE WERE KILLED

3.28

TIMES MORE OFTEN THAN WHITE PEOPLE

BLACK PEOPLE WERE KILLED

2.28

TIMES MORE OFTEN THAN ALL OTHER RACES COMBINED

VICE NEWS 2015

In the wake of the nationwide protests that gave birth to the 'Black Lives Matter' movement, roughly 24 states have instituted at least 40 new laws or policies in place to stem officer-perpetrated violence and killings. In some cities, police departments have outfitted officers with bodycams to increase accountability, while in others cops have been trained in impartial and community-based policing.

Unfortunately in the data gleaned on civilian deaths by police in the following 12 months, there were only 22 cases where officers were indicted or charged with crimes for killing citizens, while a significant number (around 257 deaths) had been either ruled an accident or found that the officers were justified in their use of fatal force! Obama's analysis stands! Change is a very slow train coming!

Cover up:

For more than a decade, government agencies were stating that there is *no hard data* to determine how many citizens are killed by police across the country each year. The only annual report made available was the FBI report of "Justifiable Homicides" which showed about 400 deaths per year since 2009 attributed to "The killing of a felon by a law enforcement officer in the line of duty."

But after the death of Mike Brown in Ferguson, Missouri last year (2014) the combination of public pressure and relentless media scrutiny led to the Bureau of Justice Statistics (BJS) to release a report detailing that at least *928 people had been killed by police annually over the previous eight years* — more than doubling the number reported by the FBI!

Black Lives Matter Movement:

After the Ferguson shooting and other killings of unarmed Afro-Americans, the public continuously demanded answers as well as better statistics. Such humiliations and a lack of perceived change led to the formation of the *Black Lives Matter* movement. But we then saw further aggravations and incidences such as: tasering a handcuffed man 20 times until he died; Chicago police caught on video tasering an Afro-American man to death whilst being held in custody. Add to this behaviours such as: Trump supporters viciously punch and kick a 'Black Lives Matter' protester at a rally and the sneering of Trump himself, virtually condoning such action! Then followed by several 'Black Lives Matter Protesters' being shot by white supremacists in Minneapolis and D.Trump's failure to denounce the Ku Klux Klan. Well, what hope? He wishes to remove the 'gun-free zones' and endorses that all teachers should have a gun in the schoolroom or university lecture theatre! In fact all Americans should carry a gun at all times (does that include Afro-Americans and Hispanics?)

The recent shooting of a black man in Minnesota, Louisiana by police after pulling the driver over for a faulty tail light shocked people around the world. However it must be stated clearly that both the driver and the police were carrying handguns at the time, so what can we expect? In another incident we saw a very large police officer struggling with a black man on the ground. We see his hand reach for his weapon in a rear holster, then fire several shots into the man's chest. Both these incidents were *unwarranted first degree murder!* The aftermath resulted in a sniper killing five police in Dallas, Texas and fierce and violent demonstrations across America. I do not condone the killing of police; in fact I have said often that the punishment for killing a police officer must be a mandatory death sentence! But let us disarm everyone. ***Guns off cops guns off everyone!*** In order to determine the society it wants to become, there must first be acknowledgement in '*what America is today*'. Then and only then can one move forward!

Racism by Afro-Americans, whites or any group is intolerable. It is not hard to find websites spewing out anti-Semitic or anti-black filth based in America. It is hard to understand why and how they are permitted to exist... certainly not under freedom of speech? All of these things point to a malaise, an illness of the society itself that can only lead to more violence. There is no immediate quick-fix to overcome these problems. But a closer look at the media, especially what is dished up for children might help. Better schools for everyone with a recognizable *value set* that communities can adhere to and an equal opportunity for all to advance to their full potential. All this of course demands money as well as thought and therein lays another seemingly insurmountable mountain! How to get more money into public institutions and make them serve the people as they should? It takes a 'will' for change! There are heaps more important words in the Bill of Rights and the Constitution than the ridiculous "second amendment".

The alternative is an imitation of the current Israel-Palestine situation of mutual mistrust and hatred... leading to where?

[I interrupt my writing progress here as my 7 year old son has just asked me to assist him with downloading and printing Slug Terra images... naturally he has chosen guns and similar futuristic weapons!]

Civilians Killing Cops:

With the rise in the reports of people being killed by police, much has been made of the danger police face every day in the line of duty. It has become the easy explanation in an attempt to justify the

Officers Feloniously Killed

	Deaths
2004	57
2005	55
2006	48
2007	57
2008	41
2009	48
2010	56
2011	72
2012	48
2013	27
Total	**509**

Source:
FBI Annual Reports: Law Enforcement Officers Killed and Assaulted

erosion of civil rights in the name of job safety for those who "protect and serve" and of course for all to carry a weapon! Across the whole

112

nation we see on average about 50 officers being killed whilst on duty. This is equivalent to about 3.3 deaths per 100,000 making policing one of the safer occupations in the country by far. Compare to: Loggers 91.3; Taxi drivers 17.8; Bartenders 16.4

Civilians Killing Civilians:

We see during the run up to the presidential elections in 2016 demonstrations heralding the dismay of the people with republican D.Trump. One of the placards held high read "90 Americans shot each day- time to end the killings!" At first I could not believe that that number could possibly be true as it amounted to roughly a little over 30000 gun deaths plus injuries per year, until I went searching for the statistics! ... and here they are:

Gun Violence Archive:

Gun Violence 2014

total number of deaths	12585
number of injuries	23041
deaths in mass shootings *	280
claimed home invasion	2610
claimed defensive use	1586

* defined as an incident kills or injures four or more people

Gun Violence 2015

total number of deaths	13399
number of injuries	26990
deaths in mass shootings	475
claimed home invasion	2346
claimed defensive use	1959

injured 1870

According to the Brady Campaign to Prevent Gun Violence:

total deaths:	32 500
total injuries:	76 000

89 people die each day from gun violence. Of these:
31 are murdered
55 kill themselves
2 are killed accidentally
1 is killed by the police
1 intent is unknown

208 people survive each day after being shot. Of these:
151 are shot in an assault
10 survive a suicide attempt
45 are shot accidentally
2 are shot by the police

The first thing to observe is that there is conflicting numbers here- in fact a huge discrepancy! Compare 13399 with 32500 total deaths and again 26990 with 76000 injuries! The accepted government figure for all gun deaths in 2015 was around 13500.

How the US compares: The number of gun murders per capita in the US in 2012 (the most recent year for comparable statistics) was nearly 30 times that in the UK, at 2.9 per 100 000 compared with just 0.1 per 100 000

Of all the murders in the US in 2012, 60% were by firearm compared with 31% in Canada, 18.2% in Australia, and just 10% in the UK. (Source: **UNODC**)

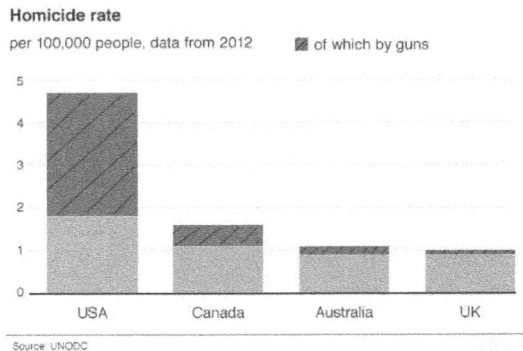

Homicide rate
per 100,000 people, data from 2012   ▨ of which by guns

Source: UNODC

It has been observed that, in the US, so many people die annually from gunfire that the death toll between 1968 and 2011 eclipses all wars ever fought by the country. According to research by Politifact, there were about 1.4 million firearm deaths in that period, compared with 1.2 million US deaths in every conflict from the War of Independence to Iraq!

According to *Brady Campaign to Prevent Gun Violence in America:*

On average, more than 89 people die from gun violence every day.

Two-thirds of those gun deaths are suicides which are three times more likely to happen if there is a gun in the home. This equates to a staggering 32500 deaths per year in total or 10.64 per 100 000!

Also, more than 90 percent of Americans support the expansion of Brady background checks to all gun sales? However, only 60 percent of gun sales occur with a background check, the other 40 percent happen with no questions asked. Furthermore, about 90 percent of crime guns are traced to only 5 percent of gun dealers. Additionally 1.7 million children live in a home with an unlocked or loaded gun, and yet our elected representatives in Congress continue to fail to act!

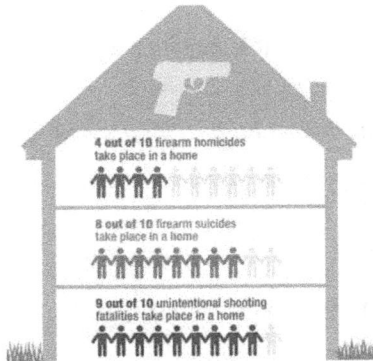

4 out of 10 firearm homicides take place in a home

8 out of 10 firearm suicides take place in a home

9 out of 10 unintentional shooting fatalities take place in a home

And further:

Every Day on Average (that is between ages 0-19):

Every day 48 children and teens are shot in murders, assaults, suicides & suicide attempts, unintentional shootings, and police intervention.

Every day, 7 children and teens die from gun violence:

5 are murdered

2 kill themselves.

Every day, 41 children and teens are shot and survive:

31 shot in an assault

1 survives a suicide attempt

8 are shot unintentionally

Asking this simple question is an important step every parent can take to help keep their child safe, and possibly save their child's life!

"Is it a smart and sensible idea to keep guns in the family home?"

In One Year on Average (that is between ages 0-19)

Around 17,500 American children and teens are shot in murders, assaults, suicides & suicide attempts, unintentional shootings, or by police intervention.

2,677 kids die from gun violence:

1,671 children and teens are murdered

827 children and teens kill themselves

124 children and teens killed unintentionally

24 are killed by police intervention

30 die but the intent was unknown

14,822 kids survive gun injuries:

11,420 are injured in an attack

280 survive a suicide attempt

3,061 are shot unintentionally

62 are shot in a police intervention

In America, 1 out of 3 homes with kids have guns and nearly 1.7 million children live in a home with an unlocked, loaded gun. *"Talking to children about the dangers of firearms is not enough! We need to get firearms out of our homes!"*

Brady Campaign
To Prevent Gun Violence

Further Comparisons with other Countries:

Interesting to see which are the 'safer countries' to live in, assuming you don't wish to be shot by a gun! For all the bad stats for the US one is even far less safe living in certain Latin American countries. I wonder what the gun sales are like in those countries and how easy it is to obtain a gun if you have the loolah! Again I lay considerable blame at the feet of corporations manufacturing weapons. The easier it is to sell then the bigger the profits that come rolling in! Obviously I have omitted current hot spots where wars are being fought such as Syria, Iraq, Afghanistan and the Ukraine! I have no figures for Africa and Asia. All the various players do not seem to have difficulties in acquiring weapons and ammunition.

But whatever the statistics in these other countries, it is of more use to point to those with relatively low deaths by guns and ask the question "why is it so?" The answer generally is tighter gun laws

Firearm Deaths per 100 000 Population

United States	10.64
Canada	2.22
Australia	0.35
UK	0.10
France	3.01
Germany	2.76
South Africa	21.51
Latin America and West Indies:	
Honduras	64.80
Venezuela	50.90
El Savadore	46.85
Jamaica	39.74
Guatemala	36.36
Colombia	28.14
Brazil	19.03
Mexico	11.17

with a disciplined regime for the rules of sales and registration! Again this falls back on the political will and demands from the populace. The higher statistics exhibited for Latin countries provides no excuse for the US which, after all, is supposed to be a leading example of a civilized democracy. Enough is enough!

The two graphs below were an attempt by an enthusiastic gun association to show that deaths by firearms in America are not too bad in comparison with other nations. The weakness in this pathetic argument is "who do we wish to compare ourselves with? ... the more civilised or the less civilised?"

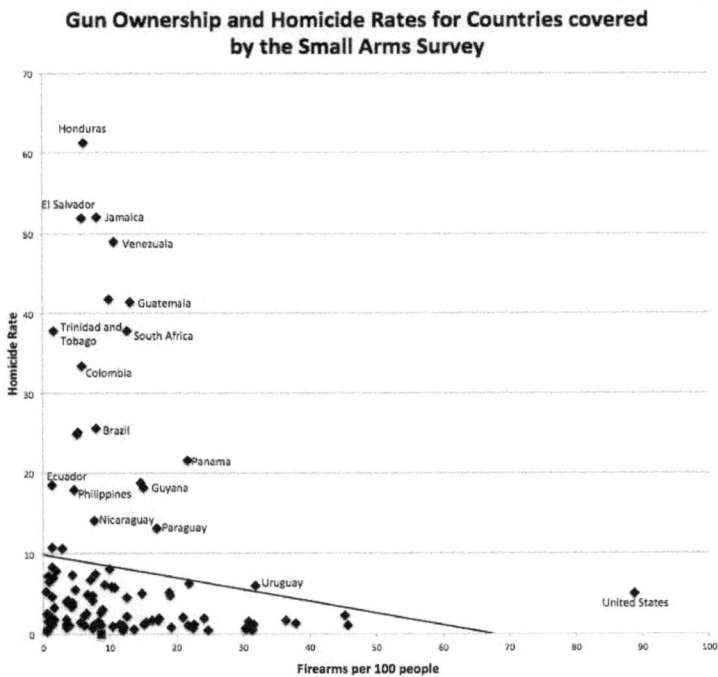

Gun Ownership and Homicide Rates for Countries covered by the Small Arms Survey

Homicide Rates for Developed Countries
(OECD 2011 or latest year)

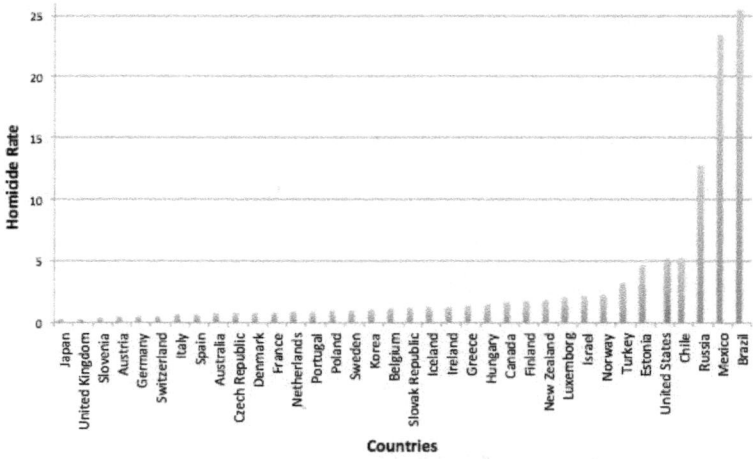

Death in Australia

The Port Arthur massacre in 1996 transformed gun control legislation in Australia. 35 people were killed and 23 wounded when the gunman opened fire on shop owners and tourists with two semi-automatic rifles. The Port Arthur perpetrator said he bought his firearms from a gun dealer without holding the required firearms licence. Prime Minister John Howard took the gun law proposals developed from the report of the 1988 National Committee on Violence and convinced the States to adopt them under a National Firearms Agreement. The proposals included a ban on all semi-automatic rifles and all semi-automatic and pump-action shotguns, and a tightly restrictive system of licensing and ownership controls. The gun buy-back scheme started on 1 October 1996 and concluded on 30 September 1997. The government bought back and destroyed nearly 1 million firearms.

We have had our Hoddle street massacre and our Port Arthur massacre over the past 3 decades and more, but due to the consequential gun laws imposed by a sensible government, deaths by firearms is still relatively low in this country. Deaths by police shootings are also low but this is still not satisfactory. Considering the statistics one might pose the question "why do cops need a handgun in Australia at all?" This is not to say that police have not been murdered or that they are not shot at occasionally, but the statistics do not merit that the police need to carry a gun. Yes, in certain circumstances as with the Lindt café quasi-terrorist event in Sydney (Nov. 2014) one needs to bring in some 'specials' with arms, but I do not feel it is necessary most of the time. The only advantage is that it gives the officer with a side-arm a semblance of added power. Most Australians feel strongly intimidated when confronted with a gun toting cowboy cop... and the author does especially. On interviewing one or two police that carry a handgun (the latest Smith & Wesson or Glock usually), they say that they prefer to feel safe and have the opportunity for a quick and decisive response when under threat. I don't think many police carried a gun in the 1950s but had the comforting knowledge that if a policeman was murdered, it most likely carried the death penalty! Now that the death penalty has been abolished, this air of protection has evaporated! (Mind you, it is the author's opinion that Australians do in fact currently support the death penalty in an off-handed way. They see no injustice in the death penalty eventually falling upon tens of thousands of young Australians due to heroine or ice addiction leading to suicide or deaths by extremely violent crime!)

Oh no, to dish out the death penalty to persons importing container loads of these drugs is seen to be inhumane and a confrontation to Australian values and civil liberties. In fact we even have the audacity to castigate neighbouring countries struggling with severe drug problems that exercise their sovereign right to take those measures to try to reduce the problem. But I am drifting... let's get back to the thrust!

Illegal guns and the importation of these into Australia are on the increase and one finds a strong correlation between illegal guns and the importation and distribution of drugs. Mexican drug cartels have infiltrated Australia and are supplying bikies, Middle Eastern gangs and Asian triads with cocaine and ice, according to new reports. These cartels have made Australia a prime target because of "significantly higher" drug prices in Australia compared to the US and South America, according to a University of Canberra report. It found that a kilogram of cocaine in Australia can fetch up to $350,000, while the same amount would fetch around only $73,000 in the United States.

"Their presence threatens to not only increase the supply of illicit drugs in Australia but encourage turf wars and increase the amount of guns in the country" associate professor Dr Anthea McCarthy-Jones said. According to a 2015 United Nations report, Mexico is the world's largest producer of ice. According to the NSW Bureau of Crime Statistics and Research drug importation offences in NSW alone have steadily increased by around 11 percent each year for the past 10 years.

(Having said this, recently container loads of ice have arrived here from China... an act of war!)

Further attempts to impose new and tighter gun laws in Australia are opposed by various shooting fraternities such as Firearms Owners Association of Australia as well as certain political parties such as the Liberal Democratic Party and the Shooters, Fishers and Farmers Party.

John Howard enacted sweeping changes in 1996 but has again recently stated that there is still room for a further tightening of the laws. Certain semi-automatic and self-loading rifles and shotguns were banned. Firearm licence applicants had to show genuine reason for having a gun, and the federal government initiated a massive gun buyback scheme that removed 700,000 firearms from circulation. Twenty years later the success of Mr Howard's gun reforms can be measured in the number of lives they've saved... however there is constant pressure to relax these laws. Australia must remain resilient to such pressure; we can never afford to be complacent! It is not sensible to allow children to use a firearm even under strict adult supervision.

The full impact of a firearm is not readily appreciated by the immature mind and can lead to undesirable consequences. Again, I see firearm control better administered under Federal Law than left to State and Territory Law. This would diminish the weaker stances taken by some states such as WA and Queensland!

Handguns should be available to gun club members only where these guns are locked away safely and held at the gun club building! We don't want handguns on our streets! In October 2002 a commerce student killed two fellow students at Monash University in Victoria with pistols he had acquired as a member of a shooting club. The gunman, Huan Yun Xiang, was acquitted of crimes related to the shootings due to mental impairment.

A current problem is with such pieces as the Adler rifle where, with modification to the magazine, may fire off dozens of bullets in rapid succession. A sensible inclusion to current law would be a mandatory jail sentence of up to 36 months for any person found to have modified a gun or its magazine! There are currently people brazenly making these modifications and thus further endangering the public. NSW has already introduced legislation against firearms to be manufactured using 3D printers and milling machines for anyone without an appropriate license.

There has been excessive media hype about potential terrorism in Australia but statistics clearly show that drugs and ordinary Australians are the key perpetrators of heinous gun related crime! After the Lindt cafe deaths, Senator David Leyonhjelm of the Liberal Democrats labelled Australia a country of "disarmed victims"... typical rubbish from the loony extreme right!

In New South Wales there have been three gun amnesties in 2001, 2003 and 2009. Around 63,000 handguns were handed in during the first two amnesties and over 4,323 handguns were handed in during the third amnesty. During the third amnesty 21,615 firearm registrations were received by the Firearms Registry. The surrendered firearms were all destroyed. These amnesties need to be organized across the whole nation!

Table: Various Causes of Death in Australia- (year in brackets)

Police Shootings (2008-2011)	Fatal: 14	Non-fatal:	0
Police Shootings (2014)	Fatal: 10	Non-fatal:	2

Road Deaths (2014)   1153

Murders (2013)   Male 157   Female 92

Firearm Related Deaths (2013)   205

Homicides by Gun (2013)   35

Drug Related Deaths (2014)   1750

Population 2014: approx. 22.5 million

As you can see, homicides by firearms are low in Australia (the USA figures per 100000 are around 12 times greater). However, as mentioned, this figure is on the increase albeit gradually. Police shootings are extremely low but one might still determine as unacceptable! Death by drug overdose or road accident taken together is 14 times more likely than being shot dead in Australia. Among those deaths by a drug overdose, males are 3 times more likely to die of a drug overdose than females.

125

In 2013, the Australian Institute of Criminology released a report detailing fatal police shootings between 1989 and 2011. In that period, police fatally shot 105 people across the country. The victims were almost entirely male and 60% were between 20 and 39 years of age.

Of those persons shot by police, 42% were suffering a mental illness at the time of the shooting. Schizophrenia was the most common illness suffered (59% of those with a mental illness). In at least one of the recent Queensland shootings, the person shot was allegedly a sufferer of mental illness. The UK primarily operates on the model of general duties police not being armed. They rely instead on backup from armed response teams if the need for lethal force arises; authorisation to use lethal force is vested in senior officers. The benefits of this system are clear. Between 2008 and 2012, England and Wales combined had just nine fatal police shootings, despite having a combined population more than double that of Australia.

Recently the Queensland police commissioner ordered all police to carry their firearms due to a perceived increased national security threat in the community. This message reinforces the idea that the firearm is the main use of force option! Having a knowledge of their ability to look more intimidating, is this perhaps the main reason for an increase in police brutality in Queensland in recent years?

See http://qldcops.blogspot.com.au/ "Queensland Police- a barrel with a lot of bad apples!"

Whether or not the tightening of gun laws has reduced the number of homicides in the land, there is one fact that is certain: "mass killings by automatic and semi-automatic firearms are far fewer and less likely under the new restrictions!" This is something that our brothers and sisters in America should take strong note of to rid themselves of this style of continuing carnage in American society. Also, a handgun in one's purse does not carry the guarantee of safety that so many like to tout!

A 2014 report has stated that more than 250,000 guns are on the Australian 'grey' or black markets. It also discussed the potential problem of people now using 3D printers to create guns. NSW and Victorian police, after obtaining plans to create 3D printed guns, created and tested to see if they would fire. The guns exploded during testing! An unauthorised shipment of dozens of Glock pistols was discovered by customs officers in Sydney in 2015. One can order these handguns via the internet but the chances of one reaching your post box are slim… however not impossible!

When a gun owner becomes deceased there needs to be an automatic cross-check to ensure that her/his guns are picked up by the police and not passed on to relatives or friends where they may remain unregistered. This is best performed by a central agency in Canberra. At present it is left to each state to maintain its own registries. This is OK as long as state gun registries are *linked* to a national central registry which is automatically updated daily. This is the only way to keep tabs on all legal firearms owned by clubs and members of the public. I repeat here that no handgun should be kept in a household. All handguns should be kept under lock and key at a club premise.

I have discussed my strong feelings on punishment for major illegal drug importers in my book *"Return to Animalia"*. With regard to the various crimes with guns I feel that importers, sellers and distributors of illegal firearms must be dealt with severely. If a shipment of illicit handguns or fully automatic weapons arrives on our shores, there is bound to be a receiver that is responsible for the cargo. This person or company must then receive considerable punishment under the law commensurate with the estimated damage that might have otherwise been inflicted on society. It is merely a matter of common sense! If intelligence gained can trace back to the identity of the original providers in a foreign country, all the better.

ABC Report: 3 Aug 2015

There has been a dramatic rise in the number of registered guns across New South Wales, with the biggest rises in gun ownership in Sydney's most affluent suburbs, including Neutral Bay, Pyrmont and Sydney's CBD. The latest figures obtained by the NSW Greens show there are now more than 850,000 firearms in private hands, which equates to one gun for every nine people. That is an almost 40 per cent rise since 2001!

NSW Greens MP David Shoebridge said he was so concerned about the surge that his party is going to introduce legislation that will attempt to impose limits on the number of firearms people can register.

"When you live in metropolitan parts of the state, we need a reasonable cap on the number of guns," he said.

"Why should anyone have more than two or three or at most five* guns if they live in the middle of metropolitan Sydney? That's what politicians are refusing to grasp, that most people want a cap on the number of guns that their neighbours can own."

[*Tom thinks the cap should be two!]

In 22 of the state's 600 postcodes, registered guns now outnumber people! Here is a 2015 list showing the highest number of guns owned by an individual for NSW (excluding guns by collectors and arms dealers):

Newcastle - 322

Moonbi - 313

Chifley, Eastgardens, Matraville, Little Bay, Hillsdale, La Perouse, Malabar, Phillip Bay and Port Botany - 302 each

Mosman - 278

North Sydney - 267

Alstonvale , Alstonville, Bagotville, Cabbage Tree Island, Dalwood, East Wardell, Lynwood, Meerschaum Vale, Pearces Creek, Rous, Rous Mill, Tuckombil, Uralba, Wardell and Wollongbar - 239 each

Manly - 207

Dubbo - 205

Amaroo, Boomey, Cundumbul, Molong, Euchareena, Garra, Larras Lee, The Shades and Warnecliffe - 186 each

Belrose and Davidson - 181 each

Well the author believes that that cap should be *two* firearms per registered owner and enforced *nationwide*! Whereas there is always a lot of hue and cry from gun owners, two is sufficient. (I do not include here antique weapons owned by registered collectors!) Obviously it is in the interest of gun retailers, importers and gun manufacturers to exacerbate this situation, as sales means profit! These same people do not seem to mind armed police roaming our towns and streets. Again more sales and more profit! The author begs to differ and has a far simpler notion of what he considers as *'a safe environment for a safe society!'*

Federal and State governments have recently enacted stringent anti-terror laws and widened police powers of arrest and detainment of suspected terrorists and with the age now reduced to 14 years. We have experienced in Australia two terrorist attacks where the criminal has (with assistance) obtained an illegal gun and killed someone. Both acts were perpetrated in Sydney. Without providing detailed analysis of each (which has proven to be illusive and beyond even the most accomplished) the author's opinion is that each might have been prevented with just a little more insight to the character of each of the perpetrators. Certainly the ease of which a gun was procurable placed no barrier to the intention. Together with the aforementioned mass shootings, the Australian public deserve constant improvement on gun control. This can be accomplished without severe infringement on the rights of farmers, hunters and recreational shooters. National registration and more severe penalties is the best way forward.

Incidentally, the author lives in Eastern Victoria where guns outnumber local residents significantly. I have no objection to recreational hunting and shooting but see no sense in ownership of many guns by the one person. It amazes me that gun owners occasionally display unconcealed anger at my stance and make foolish claims that "lefties wish to disarm the people!" Well, my retort is that "intelligent people wish to disarm the angry and the dangerous!" If one wishes to own a hundred fishing rods, I display no objection!

But why has there been a dramatic increase in gun ownership in NSW? I can only point to all the media hype on terrorism* in Australia which would be a joke if the trend were not true!

[* The author cannot understand why those wishing to join IS in Syria are prevented from leaving Australia? He believes that a one-way ticket is reasonable with no chance of ever returning! The charge of 'traitor' seems to have disappeared from the statutes in modern times?]

Very few police officers have been murdered in Australia. Since 1945 only nine Federal police have been deliberately killed, including the Assistant Commissioner in Canberra in January 1989.

Some 757 police have died whilst on duty since 1803 which includes service in the Pacific, wartime deaths and accidental deaths. In more recent times we witnessed two police shot dead in August 1988 in

Melbourne followed by a further two shot dead in 1998, also in Melbourne.

A Tamworth (NSW) police officer was shot and later died in March 2012.

The number of guns stolen has fallen from an average of around 4000 per year between the years 1994 to 2000, to around 1500 per year between the years 2006–2007. Rifles and shotguns are more often stolen during home burglaries. With few handguns in homes, a substantial proportion of stolen handguns are acquired from security firms and other businesses. Only 0.06% of licensed firearms are stolen in a given year, however only a small proportion of these are ever recovered. Approximately 3% of stolen guns are later connected to an actual crime or found in the possession of a person charged with a serious offence.

I give all this information to my friends in America that they may make rational decisions on their future society… one that is genuinely safer for its children and citizens generally!

Did Dan Dare? ... the New Weapons

Note: this chapter is taken, with minimal editing, from the book *"Return to Animalia"* by Tom Law.

Please bear with me and skim through:

"Former airline boss and famous French author Marc Dugain has argued that there had been a cover-up in the disappearance of Malaysian Airlines flight MH370, speculating that the passenger jet might have been hacked and shot down by the US." Dugain suspected that the plane headed towards Diego Garcia, where the US Air Force shot it down for fear of a September 11-style attack. He also noted that Inmarsat - the last organisation to receive a signal from the airliner is "very close to intelligence agencies". A British Intelligence officer apparently had cautioned Dugain against the "risks" of investigating the flight's disappearance! (... threats related back to Private Security Companies? ... refer back to earlier chapter: Are You a Private Private?)

Japanese racehorse Admire Rakti collapsed and died after pulling up distressed after the 2014 Melbourne Cup. The horse, which started a well-backed Melbourne Cup favourite, was eased out of the race on the home turn whilst in second place. He dropped dead in his stall shortly after the race. Coalition for the Protection of Racehorses (CPR... no pun intended!) spokesman said "We think the real issue is over exertion and use of the whip."

Protectionist became the first German horse to win the Melbourne Cup, taking out the $6.2 million race on cup day at Flemington. He was ridden by English jockey Ryan Moore. The British horse Araldo took fright on the way back to the mounting yard, jumping a steel rail and getting its leg caught in the barrier. Araldo was rushed to Werribee Veterinary Hospital but experts determined the injuries were too severe to recover from and was consequently put down.

The daughter-in-law of the author was brought into Box Hill hospital after collapsing in her home driveway. After two weeks convalescence a similar attack occurred and she was admitted back to same hospital. Two days later she died in the night from brain swelling. After extensive testing and post-mortem no detectable cause was diagnosed. A death certificate to this effect was issued more than six months after death. She was aged 40 years.

A team of scientists from Britain's National Physics Laboratory and Imperial College, London led by Dr. Mark Oxborrow report that they have created the first solid state maser that operates at room temperature, paving the way toward the widespread practical application of the technology (early 2012). Their breakthrough was to replace the hard, inorganic maser crystal with an organic mixed-molecular crystal, p-terphenyl doped with pentacene. The pentacene, which makes the crystal look pink, is photo-excited by yellow light.

The Laser Weapon System or LaWS is a directed energy weapon developed by the United States Navy. The weapon was installed on the *USS Ponce* for field testing in 2014. In December 2014 the United States Navy reported that the LaWS system works perfectly and further that the commander of the *USS Ponce* is authorized to use the system as a defensive weapon. (… and has commenced poncing about since?)

The LaWS is designed to be used against low-end asymmetric threats (whatever that means?) Scalable power levels allow it to be used on low-power to dazzle a person's eye to non-lethally make them turn away from a threatening posture, and increase to 30 thousand watt (30 kW) to fry sensors, burn out motors, and detonate explosive materials (and I assume fry a person to carbon also if desired!) Against a vital point on small UAVs, one can be shot down in as little as two seconds. When facing small boats, the laser would target a craft's motor to disable it and make it "dead in the water" then repeating this against others in rapid succession, requiring only a few seconds of firing per boat. Targeting the platform is more effective than individual crewmembers, although the LaWS is accurate enough to target explosive rockets if on board, whose detonations could kill the operators. *Against larger aircraft like helicopters, it is able to burn through some vital components, which would cause it to fall and crash.* Most high-energy lasers are in the *invisible* IR region. So you won't see it coming folks!

The most recent tests of LaWS are part of several rounds of testing that have occurred over the past three years. In a 2011 test, a laser weapon disabled multiple small boats launched from a US warship. In 2012, LaWS downed several drones during a naval test of the system.

Contractors of ongoing high-energy laser weapons projects include: Lockheed Martin; Northrop Grumman; Optonicus; General Atomics; Boeing; Kratos; Raytheon; BAE Systems.

A German company has brought us one step closer to the kinds of shootouts only seen in Sci-Fi films.

Düsseldorf-based Rheinmetall Defense recently tested a 50kW, high-energy laser at their proving ground facility in Switzerland. According to the company, the laser passed the test with "flying colours." (interpret that as you see fit!)

The system isn't actually a single laser but two laser modules mounted onto Revolver Gun air defence turrets made by Oerlikon and attached to additional power modules. The laser modules are 30 kW and 20 kW, but a Beam Superimposing Technology (BST) combines two lasers to focus in a "superimposed, cumulative manner" that wreaks havoc on its targets.

Table of relative laser power:

< 1 milliwatt	Class 1 laser Harmless
2 milliwatt	Class 2 laser Harmless
5 milliwat	Class 3 laser Mostly Harmless laser pointers
30 milliwatt	Class 3B laser if wavellength 400 nm to 700 nm Needs protective eyeware
400 milliwatt	Red DVD burner Needs protective eyeware
0.5 watt	Class 3B laser if wavelength > 315 nm Needs protective eyeware Medical laser
0.6 watt	Class 4 laser Will ignite combustible material Needs protective eyeware
0.7 watt	Blue Ray DVD burner
5 watt	Beam capable of igniting wood
30 watt	Low power CO2 laser
60 watt	Rock concert laser light
100 watt	CO2 laser for surgical procedures
200 watt	Industrial CO2 laser for cutting plastic and very thin metal
1 kilowatt	Capable of cutting metal plate
30 kilowatt	US Navy Laser Weapon System LaWS Directed Energy Weapon DEW
50 kilowatt	German point-defense laser system
100 kilowatt	US miltary MILSPEC directed energy weapon Weapons-grade laser

First, the system sliced through a 15mm- (~0.6 inches) thick steel girder *from a kilometre away*. Then, from a distance of two kilometres, it shot down a handful of drones as they nose-dived toward the surface at 50 meters per second.

While minuscule compared to the 200 petawatt of laser power (ten to the fifteenth watt!) that scientists in Europe plan to use for experiments (like blowing up the moon perhaps or melting a small country?), the 50kW laser seems quite ready to make a difference on the battlefield. Apart from science fiction novels, the idea of using high-energy lasers has been considered for weaponry since the mid 20th century. Countries such as the US, Russia, China, among others, are developing their own high-energy laser programs. Whether or not we hear about future demonstrations will be a matter of national security rather than technological success. I think it's safe to assume this is one arms race that's already here and blossoming! Well zapp me dead!

Where can I purchase a 'Dr. Schilling's sidearm'? Probably on the www!

Israeli defence company Elbit Systems has announced it will provide an anti-missile laser protection system for the German Air Force (you gotta be kidding me, that has to be a first!) It will be used to protect transport planes from surface to air and portable heat seeking missiles.

China has conducted two anti-satellite tests very recently, using its advanced laser technology. This was done during a recent exercise of the Peoples Liberation Army. The anti-satellite exercises were conducted using laser weapons. This was disclosed by Konstantin Sivkov, deputy head of the Moscow-based Think Tank, Academy of Geopolitical Problems, in an interview to Voice of Russia. US government sources told the Defense News that the US will keep quiet for the time being, regarding the anti-satellite tests, as it values Beijing's role as an important trade partner. However while visiting air force headquarters in Beijing, Xi, who is also head of the military, told officers "to speed up air and space integration and sharpen their offensive and defensive capabilities."

Dan Dare was once a hero. He brokered peace with alien races, pushed the frontiers of space, and saved the planet from total annihilation... repeatedly. But now, his Space Fleet has disbanded, the United Nations has crumbled, his friends scattered to the solar winds. Britain is once again the world power, but Dare, disillusioned and disappointed in his once-precious home country, has quietly retired. But there's trouble mustering in Deep Space. The H.M.S. Achilles is picking up strange signals when, suddenly, an enormous fleet of hostile ships ambushes the destroyer. As the crew struggles to stay alive, they realize with horror that the hostiles have brought a weapon of unimaginable power. Dan Dare, pilot of the future, has been called out of retirement!

Well I don't see Britain as ever again being *the world power* unless of course the rest are mutually destroyed in some high-tech nuclear cum biochemical war! The author came back from China one-eyed and wonders if he partook in some military experiment?

Was MH370 downed by a laser weapon? This plane's passengers comprised mainly ethnic Chinese and again one might put the question was there any relationship between this and the Malaysian aircraft brought down over the Ukraine- MH17? A wild speculation is that this was an agreed pay-back (i.e between China and its ally Russia)! BUK-M1 missile manufacturer Almaz-Antey chief engineer Malisvskiy has claimed that evidence indeed points to an 'older' type of this missile, but claims the Ukraine army also had almost 1000 of these at the time of the downing.

If you watch the replay of the Melbourne Cup race for 2014, you will see a vehicle come into sight inside the last turn with a lot of equipment on it. Just at that moment Admire Rakti suddenly fades away. Was a new pink crystal maser weapon used on him? Was it a flag that scared Araldo not long after the end of the race or by means of a similar weapon? Romantic science-fiction speculation?

Australians have been charged from shining lasers at the police and aircraft at night time. However the beam from the new cold maser cannot be seen with the human eye. Does it follow now that mobile phones, cameras or other electronic devices may not be brought to a sporting event in the not too distant future? Probably!

Whenever the West invents new weapons, there is a mistaken belief that it brings *safety and security*. But it is not so. As we move forward with drones, robots and laser/maser weapons, all we have achieved is to give potential enemies the same ideas. They will be emulated and just bring the peoples of this world more angst as they face new high tech weapons with no possible preparedness and protection against eventual annihilation.

Did my daughter in law die of a natural cause or was it again due to a similar cowardly attack? Are the members of the Fourth Reich motor cycle club just simple thugs or are some members professionals such as physicists and engineers? I pose all these questions in the light of the

140

prevalence and pervasiveness of new high technology weapons that are now an adjunct to the final destruction and collapse of our world with no ultimate winner. Helter Skelter!

We were told recently that Australia Post might soon be delivering parcels to remote places by drones. It seems this technology is the future with the air filled with delivery drones flitting here and there in place of motorised vans that are limited to the road system. Of course the military, especially the US forces have been using drones in its various wars presently in different parts of the world to deliver high explosives to their enemies. Unfortunately we have seen innocent civilians blown up in villages in Pakistan and Afghanistan where the targets were meant to be al Qaida or Taliban terror groups or individuals. Up until end June 2016 approximately 2500 enemy fighters were claimed to have been killed with more than 100 civilians killed by drones. However, the civilian casualty rate is believed to be up to four times this number with many more wounded.

One wonders if even political dissidents (so labelled) might become targets within America and other Western countries by these drones in the future. It all fits to the *Theory of the Organelle* where we reach the next stage in evolution of living things… the planet becomes a single living entity or organism where the good and well behaved cells are allowed to live and carry out their subordinate functions whilst the bad, the so-called germs, are exterminated. But who will make the decisions as to life or death? Why the controllers at their desks in the Pentagon or their equivalent in Beijing or Moscow of course!

Are we being desensitised to the horrors of war and destruction by the media, movies and computer simulation games? Many young people spend too much time at the controls of various aps that simulate killing, bombing and annihilation of 'the enemy'. I see *Mobile Strike* advertised on TV with what sounds like Arnie Schwarzenegger's voice! The older generations grew up with cowboys and Indians, World War II, Vietnam and now movies about the fight against Islamic terrorism. Futuristic fantasies like Star Wars and their ilk still focus on the eternal battle of 'good versus evil'. But are we now saturated? TV has spawned hundreds of cop shows most of which involve guns and the application of guns. When we see on the news thousands of refugee families herded into tent cities with alarming peeks at their former cities bombed to rubble, are we moved? If not, I make the hypothesis that "it is coming". What do I mean? I mean that it is likely coming to us all. The reason? The reasons are clearly laid out in this writing!

'All I ask of you' whatever your place in society is that you place the highest value on peace and love of your fellow man and be *traitor* to actions that damage our fragile existence whilst you live. God is above humanity, but humanity is above the largess, desires and whims of nations. And family will always be the bedrock of humanity. Intelligent scientists perceiving to be 'more intelligent than God' have wrought ploughshares into swords. Their petty national pride and lack of moral judgement has paid a disservice to all of humankind and limited the planet to countable days before its demise. The *'moment of phut'* is near!

Alternatively we could grasp the *'new age of enlightenment'*, a Confucian and Taoist choice that guarantees the continuation of human civilisation and Earth environment!

Grim Reaper… coming your way soon!

Each week we see, as part of the news, the prices of essential economic markers such as an ounce of gold, a barrel of oil, a tonne of iron ore etc. Also we see the relative currency values of a country's currency against the US dollar. These fluctuations depend on supply and demand with an overlay of confidence in markets tempered by factors such as wars. Occasionally we see sudden crashes either in a single nation or sometimes in a geographical collection of nations. At present we see turmoil in the Middle East, particularly in Iraq and Syria. However other nearby countries continue to supply oil to world markets and, despite these conflagrations, the price of oil has been depressed. Iran has played a significant role here as it has stepped down from its nuclear weapons program* and embargoes have been dissipated. Naturally it is keen to make up for lost revenue over the previous decade and thus there is plenty of oil to be had just now at the beginning of 2016. The US has increased greatly its domestic production of shale oil thus reducing its level of imports.

[* albeit the regime doesn't recognise any treaty after ten years! In a childish way the regime continues to deny the Holocaust and trivializes it in an inflammatory and abhorrent manner. In May 2016 it staged yet another Holocaust-themed cartoon contest that mocked the Nazi genocide of six million Jews during World War II. The **International Holocaust Cartoon Contest** was a cartoon competition sponsored by the Iranian newspaper *Hamshahri*, to denounce what it called "Western hypocrisy on freedom of speech".]

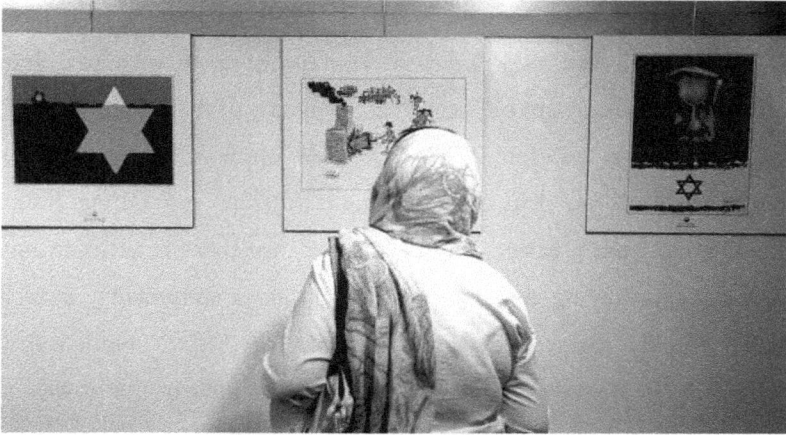

A cynic might point to the current war in Syria/Iraq as an exercise in capitalism at its worst, where Iran and other Shiite Muslim groups wish to traverse these countries to get an oil and gas pipeline into Europe. The predominantly Sunni Muslim Saudi Arabia would not wish to see such competition flower and consequently might

Adel al_Jubeir

covertly be tempted to support any war that would frustrate such ambitions. Perhaps I am oversimplifying a very complex situation? The

Kurdish peoples seem to have been the main ground force to have confronted ISIL but they have no country of their own and Iran together with Turkey are unlikely to concede any of their lands to bring such a dream to fruition. Whatever one's opinion on the mess at present, there is no denying that Sunni Muslims are killing Shiite Muslims on a daily basis. Why is this so? Are there benefits to any third party in having two major sects of Islam continually at each other's throats? So called military attacks on Shiite communities, particularly in Baghdad have almost always resulted in the deaths of great numbers of women and children. The people of Iraq have experienced this for nearly twenty years.

Again we see America and Russia at odds on which groups to support in Syria (financially and militarily) with the extreme loss of civilian lives as a consequence. Each has tried to upstage the other clambering for some moral high ground but despite their gesturing, we see between 500 000 and one million deaths and more than four million people displaced. ISIL has never had more than about 20000 ground troops in the area and it is hard to fathom that they were able to control so much area despite coalition bombings daily for almost a year! Syria puts blame on Qatar and shadowy figures in Turkey and Saudi Arabia with plenty of cash to spare. Had the US not armed Syrian rebel groups then the extent of civilian deaths may never have reached current sickening figures. The big and powerful countries such as the US, Russia, the UK and China seem to be (from this writer's perspective) to be more a causal influence than a panacea to cure all ills! Despite keeping Western ground troops out of the region, there is still a risk of a World conflagration being born from this petty war.

Libya, Egypt, Tunisia and Yemen have all suffered and continue to suffer their own civil conflicts. Israel and Palestine have sporadic incidents (although the disgraceful Gaza annihilation was more than sporadic) as does Lebanon. Several African countries with Muslim extremists are also suffering internal conflicts.

A cynic might also pose the question "where does all the money and weapons come from to promulgate and exacerbate these continuing confrontations?"

Answer: "from the sale of oil and from the warehouses of the armament producers and sellers of course!"

Oil is energy. Countries need vast amounts of energy to drive their societies and economies. Any tinkering with the chain of supply sends tremors and repercussions across vital economies.

Saudi Arabia, although recently expressing its wish to commence to diversify its reliance on oil alone, can almost be said to have an infinite supply of oil. Regardless of its push into other sectors of commerce, oil sales are unlikely to ever decline in volume and will continue to buoy up its economy for a very long time to come.

And to disregard Russia and China along with western economies as not being capitalistic (with regard to arms sales) is to cloud the mind and make a grave error. Dozens upon dozens of countries clamber for a piece of the military cake where opportunistic monopolies in armaments are continuously out there selling and foisting their wares on those foolish enough to feel the need for them. Many of these international companies, at the base line of morality, have little or no loyalty to any particular party or nation but see profit and survival as their lodestone. They have tunnel vision. They are unstoppable. They have no care for human civilisation, the planetary environment or the screams of the dying. In fact, like a sovereign nation, they are an entity in themselves motivated by greed and survival. This can only be achieved through continuous production of their products and, most important of all, sales figures. Their accountants are shut away with computer screens spitting out numbers and forecasts with no concept at all of the world reality of their actions. Their greatest fear is of 'full warehouses with stagnated shipments!' If there is a pallet with ammunition, tanks, rockets or guns... it has to be moved! The life blood and nurture of a section of society is dependent on the death, misery and exploitation of another. Those in the armament trades of the world are the mistletoe and leaches feeding off the innocent blood in the world society of humanity! I, Tom Law, said that!

Interesting that the British "Chilcot Report", an in-depth inquiry into Britain's participation in the 2003 invasion of Iraq under Prime Minister Tony Blair (along with America's President Bush and Australia's John Howard) fell just short of declaring the whole exercise as illegal! In the words of Sir John Chilcot: "We have concluded that the UK chose to join the invasion of Iraq before the peaceful options for disarmament had been exhausted. Military action at that time was not a last resort. We have also concluded that (i) The judgements about the severity of the threat posed by Iraq's weapons of mass destruction were presented with a certainty that was not justified. (ii) Despite explicit warnings, the consequences of the invasion were underestimated. The planning and preparations for Iraq after Saddam Hussein were wholly inadequate. (iii) The Government failed to achieve its stated objectives."

I have said this elsewhere and repeat again:

"The Russian invasion of Afghanistan in the 1980's followed by the armed and financial support by America to the rebel forces in that country coupled with the incursions of the West into Iraq from 2003 onwards plus further, the meddling by both Russia and the West into Syria since 2014 have each contributed in no small way to the creation of terror groups such as al Qaeda and Islamic State! The outcome of these decisions has been the destruction of village communities, whole cities and the advent of tens of millions of homeless refugees. Instead of solving a couple of problems, we have created an almost insoluble problem of gigantic proportion!"

Climate

Climate change and the warming of the planet are attributed to the continual increase of green house gases from human activity, particularly the production of carbon dioxide from the burning of fossil fuels. These are consumed in fuels for the various forms of transportation, the production of metals (particularly iron and steel) as well as a host of other industries producing things such as concrete and glass to name but two more.

CO_2 ppm   Cape Grim Tasmania

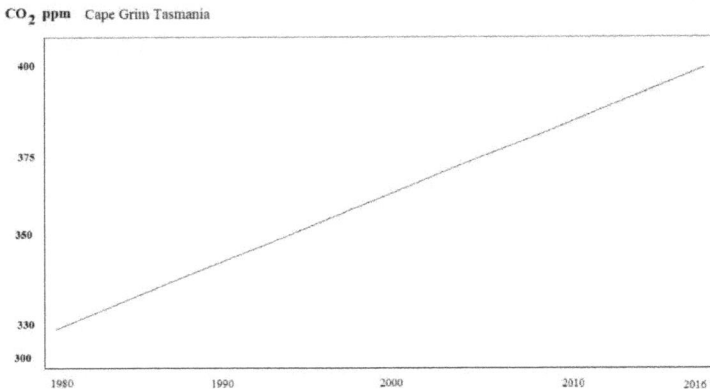

For the climate change sceptics here is a CSIRO graph of CO_2 concentrations measured at Cape Grim in Tasmania. You would expect this part of the world to be the cleanest... well CO_2 seems to be evenly distributed around the world apart from above densely populated cities. We have reached the 400 ppm level and the trend is continuing to rise. CH_4 has reached 1800 ppb and N_2O 328 ppm as of February 2016.

[ppm: parts per million by mass;   ppb: parts per billion by mass]

Does war have an effect on climate? Well at the extreme, if nuclear weapons were used the planet would soon be uninhabitable with just a few silverfish and microbes surviving. What about current wars? Well we see a lot of infrastructure in Syria, Iraq, Yemen, Libya and Gaza recently destroyed. Remembering that iron, steel, concrete and glass all produce CO_2 as a by-product in their manufacture, then the rebuilding of cities has an effect on climate. All explosions produce heat energy and oxides of nitrogen which go into the atmosphere. Deforestation in the Vietnam War would have placed some stress on the atmosphere initially. But by far the greatest effect would be in the very production of armaments and military hardware especially those requiring large amounts of steel and other metals such as tanks and warships.

Chemical processes to make plastic explosives also require energy. This in turn has its own effect, albeit small. Electrical energy is still produced mainly by the burning of fossil fuel whilst alternatives are slowly coming into play. Thus all processes involving chemical change which in turn require electrical energy, contributes to greenhouse emissions. The transportation of armaments to places of need or to storage facilities again requires energy. Is it not better to use this energy for producing and storing useful products that humans can utilise to better the quality of their lives?

The whole of the armaments business... and it is a business, produces a lot of waste as well as using up valuable energy. And for what? Well, to hasten extreme climate change of course! Another 5^0 increase in mean global temperature is about all the ecosystem will tolerate before a complete collapse and an end to all the higher forms of life. Algae and silverfish may survive to start over!

Extreme Politics and the Place of Religion

The King John-uns of the world with their total control of the people are a menace and a danger to peace and stability. The political extremists that resort 'to the last' all that is available to them in an attempt to foist their point of view on others are also a menace. Therein lays the conundrum. Violence and war seem to be part of the human character, part of survival of the tribe which we have experienced for all past time! Can we ever move forward and escape this intrepid tight rope of life to a more peaceful and safer environment where killing is no more? Certainly with the application of law we might be able to do away with violent solutions to problems between sovereign states. But this can never happen whilst international corporations covertly wish to promote conflict for the sake of profit! These new unregulated sovereign corporations need to be brought to heel. They, in many cases, are the enemy of the free peoples of the planet and some radical changes to the way we all act and think are necessary if we are to take responsibility for their eventual demise.

But how to change the thinking of an engineer or scientist that works on a new chemical to produce a cheaper or more efficient bomb? The workers on the assembly line of fighter aircraft? The inventor of a new laser weapon that can tear apart the moon? The quantum physicist that can place all the listening and watching technology onto the head of a fly?

How can the creative talents of our best and brightest be steered away from weaponry? Tom doesn't have the answer... I'm sorry. But herein is the possible way of the future or at least an alternative way for a better future!

The famed astrophysicist and cosmologist in the wheelchair- Dr Stephen Hawking - has warned us of the greatest threat to humanity in the future: that is the production of machines with memory and thinking powers vastly greater and infinitely faster than the human brain. You see, the current collective knowledge of our current society is a squillion times greater than the capacity of our individual brains to hold! Are we on the foolish road to our own demise by the construction of clever devices? Will we outsmart ourselves to the extent of self-redundancy? Probably!

[I did mention this in previous writings where I proposed that this future scenario is unavoidable, being an essential part of the cosmological theory of evolution!]

Absolutes: The theory of absolutes is highly related to mathematics, where the highest beauty of form is in perfection of structure and shape. We see this in the natural world in crystals and jewels. The underlying principal also includes atomic structure where there is a continuity of perfection in geometrical shape repeated. Perhaps this is inherent in our unconscious psychological makeup and cannot be avoided. In politics and religion humans often strive for agreement and uniformity. Once we have an overview of what we consider is correct, righteous and near to perfect, we wish to cling to it and even worse, foist it upon others. This cohesiveness brings us comfort (though to Tom, no small element of boredom) and a sense of belonging to the group. It is the very core of extreme ideologies such as National Socialism, Communism and Christian or Islamic Extremism. Nirvana then is the acceptance of absolutes that are unquestionable, incontrovertible or having infinite inertia (another word, actually two words, for God). Maybe it's nice to be a cube... but then again how about a ragged tree? The state of nirvana may be intoxicating for some but, when carried away to the extreme, allows them to perform the most horrendous deeds or inflictions of immorality upon others (as, historically, the aforementioned political groups have demonstrated). It is a question in itself and may be relegated to pure philosophy so abstract that it shows or exhibits a complete departure of what it means to be human!

This is the dilemma of us intelligent monkeys. To follow a creed or leader to the nth degree will lead us into momentary perfection but then conflict with others wishing to bring us down.

What is the essence of being human? I think we will always need the struggle and challenges that keep us occupied. At the same time we need to exercise our creative sides to produce something of beauty and thus providing satisfaction. We need closeness to other humans in what we term love... that is a mutual dependence. To give without seeking reward is the highest of human qualities. To aid or assist another human in need is also a virtuous quality. To guide and protect our young is what separates us from lesser life forms. To seek compromise in dispute is a safer bet for survival of all than violence. Unfortunately our survival instincts (but may here relate to a sense of justice) will lead us to violence on occasion and that's just the way it is! But the realisation that the planet and its resources are finite should assist us in finding solutions without violence... that is if we are sensible!

Stress from the Refugees

Libya is a country in turmoil. After the fall of the Col. Gadaffi regime (with strong assistance from the US and the UK I might add) we see a never ending civil war with two governments at extreme west and east of the nation. It is often the case that the CIA and MI5, working as a team, feel that it is the righteous and proper thing to do to topple dictators in other countries so that MacDonald's, Coca-cola, KFC and all the other icons of the West may move in to create a hazy image of a western-style democracy. The weakness of this strategy is that it cannot predict what really is going to happen to the people and society that has been interfered with! Iraq is a classic example where, after toppling Saddam Hussein, the country has never recovered to a stable society. Maiming and killing seem to be a daily scenario. It has become a society of little hope, its youth bleeding on the sidewalks of its cities, hatred between religious factions everywhere. The lesson to be learned: *"we cannot apply our sense of democracy and definition of civilisation to alien cultures... these have been proven recipes for disaster and even disintegration of those societies meddled with!"* US foreign policy in the latter half of the 20th century and the first two decades of the 21st century has been a total failure and brought havoc in the world... the very opposite to its noble intentions! The rubble and ruins of a city such as Kobane in northern Iraq is somehow seen as a success?

I understand the strong stance against communism and the sacrifices by western forces in Korea, Malaysia and elsewhere were worth the effort. The problem with trying to prop up the failing regime in Vietnam was that (i) they (the Vietnamese) were sick of being a colony and (ii) the geography was different to Korea in that it was not a peninsular and shared a border with China.

Both these elements proved the task to be too difficult.

Coming back to Libya and Africa generally, we now see it as a stepping off point for hundreds of thousands of refugees from failing countries on that continent making their way to Europe seeking some utopia or at least something better. This has been greatly exacerbated by the flood of refugees fleeing wars in Syria, Iraq, Afghanistan and the Middle East generally as well as from poorer states such as Bangladesh, India and Pakistan. This year (2016) is crunch time for Europe. It can only be the application of harsh policies to cease this influx, however difficult to impose if catastrophe is to be averted. A greater combined naval presence along the North African coast and in the Aegean is perhaps necessary. Alternatively the stresses and strains in Europe will reach a calamitous point creating civil unrest. I think to date they have been tolerant and more than generous but there are limitations above which social coherence becomes threatened.

The richer nations need to do more to assist those failing nations to improve their economies which in turn will improve the conditions of life for their citizens. No easy task! But more Kalashnikovs and ammunition is not the way! In June 2016 it is estimated that there are now in excess of 60 million refugees around the world and the number continues to grow.

Naturally the Syrian and Afghani conflicts have to end. As said, the wealthier countries must continue to assist the poorer countries in Africa and elsewhere that they build better infrastructures to look after their peoples. Corruption and the wasting of money and resources need to be dealt with at the local level. Higher standards of education to the

Gaza

masses will slowly reap rewards resulting in more comfortable and affluent societies. We have seen countries such as Iraq and Iran waste all their oil dollars in purchasing war materials and hardware instead of investing more in schools, hospitals and cultural things to lift up their societies. In fact Iraq and Iran should have been model societies had it not been for their extravagance in a lengthy war in the 20th century, thus depressing the people and robbing them of hope and a good life. But the War Lords who profited from all their misery are as much to blame. Exhibitions and fares displaying expensive military hardware to reap back all the dollars spent on oil was and continues to be their game! Shame!

Commentary on the 2015 Abu Dhabi Military Expo by Stefanie Dekker for Al Jazeera: Abu Dhabi Defence Expo Draws World's Top Military Brass

It's rare to see many of the world's top military leaders in one place. But many of them showed up at the International Defence Exhibition, which opened in Abu Dhabi on Sunday.

We saw the Ukrainian delegation, in their sandy military uniforms, deep in discussion, huddled over a small table behind a cordon, with security close by.

The Jordanians marched past us. We ran to keep up, asking for an interview. They received us with a smile but no, they were too busy. How is everything? "Very good," again with a wide smile, and they were off.

We tried talking to some of the representatives of the United Arab Emirates, the host, but they didn't want to talk.

Outside, I tried to approach two officers deep in conversations - one from the Emirates and one from Greece. The Greek officer went to his superior to see if they would talk to us. But again the answer was no.

Then we came across the Libyans, looking at the military hardware on offer.

These military officers had 'Libyan National Army' on their uniforms. They belong to the UN-recognised government in Tobruk, in the east of Libya.

There are of course two rival governments in Libya, the other sanctioned by the Supreme Court, in the capital Tripoli. And both supported by a loose coalition of heavily armed fighters.

There is currently an arms embargo on Libya. Weapons may only be imported with UN Security Council Committee approval, and Libya is already drowning in military hardware.

Following the recent beheading of 21 Egyptian Coptic Christians by the Libyan affiliated wing of the Islamic State of Iraq and the Levant (ISIL), there was a call to lift the arms embargo on the UN recognised government. But that has so far not been granted. For now it seems a case of look, but don't touch.

We were waiting to talk to the Libyan Chief of Staff. But as soon as he got wind that we were from Al Jazeera, he refused. "Qatar, no," he said. He repeated more firmly, when we tried to insist.

It highlights the regional divisions here: The Tripoli government is perceived to be supported by Qatar and Turkey, whereas the Tobruk one has Egypt and the UAE on its side.

We heard the Libyans held meetings with other military leaders - Western and Arab countries.

This Expo is not just about having the latest technology when it comes to air, land and sea capability- but it's a vital networking opportunity.

The Chinese are here too, not just browsing what's on offer, but also selling, as so many other countries.

The Americans and the British have their military hardware here, in the form of some of the biggest defence companies in the world.

French and German soldiers showed off their equipment, with two French soldiers simulating a patrol around their stand.

The Sudanese President Omar al-Bashir attended the opening ceremony; he's here along with his minister of defence. And the

Sudanese also had an expanded stand this year, with more weapons and explosives on offer than what they had at the same conference two years ago.

We had a last ditch attempt to follow a delegation - once again marching through the exhibition centre in a hurry. Once I managed to catch up I realised it was the Italians.

How did they feel about the threat of ISIL made just across the Mediterranean? Everyone is concerned of course they told me. But everything is fine. Could they give us an interview? They could, but not today, as they were already behind schedule, heading to another meeting.

The deals that are signed here, and officially announced, are deals that have been in the works for a while. Nothing is last minute. What is more interesting of course is what is being discussed behind closed doors.

All very well for rich Arab countries to buy expensive fighter jets, bombs and missiles but to what purpose? These nations have contributed little in ridding their backyard of ISIL but we see Saudi Arabia keen to go in and bomb rebels in Yemen, Russia bombing rebels in Syria, each committing war crimes in the process by killing innocent civilians. But then they have many more oil dollars to purchase more weapons from the eager sales persons at these Expos! My prediction in a later chapter is that all the nations manufacturing and selling will, in the long term, bring devastation and destruction upon their own heads and the heads of the affluent societies of which they are a part. See later: *"It Will All End in Tears!"*

Australia has to date dealt harshly with refugees arriving by boat, predominantly from Indonesia. Many were turned back to Indonesia by the Australian Navy. The more inhumane aspect of the Australian solution is that many refugees and boat people have languished in camps on the island of Nauru and other offshore detention centres for three years or more. Private companies have played a role in these centres which has cost the Australian tax payer millions of dollars. Many agree with the policy, however many do not agree with the lengthy duration of internees. It might have been cheaper to have flown each back to their country of origin within the first ninety days of their arrival!

The conservative Government stated towards the end of 2015 that they would resettle around 12000 additional refugees from Syria. After six months, however, only a couple of hundred have been brought to Australia. The media have constantly stirred up feelings in the community about the possibility of terrorism but to date there have been only a couple of incidences of which, even these, have serious questions as yet unanswered. Extreme right wing morons (such as the Pauline Handsome's One White Nation Party, Rise Up Australia and

Reclaim Australia hooligans to name a few) have raised their ugly faces to denigrate all Muslims in this country which is a sad indictment and goes against the norm of Australian hospitality and welcoming to all cultures and creeds. Whilst many Australians have drifted from conventional religion, in some quarters there seems to be paranoia against the aggregation of Muslim communities and their desire to build mosques. Fear based on what? Not much! Gross ignorance perhaps?

I see no reason why the refugees will not swell to even greater numbers in the coming years as more conflicts occur around the world and failing governments fail to keep check on their country's population and standard of living. Will we eventually be shooting at

them in the water? I hope not. But we live in a crazed world where so much money and resources are wasted. This can surely only be attributed by the wrong people in political power everywhere? The processes by which one reaches a place in politics needs to be questioned. Are we being served by the best and the most intelligent? Can governments curb outrageous spending on armaments and armed forces? Can the pressure from the manufacturers to sell their goods be redirected to things society needs? Big business (and BIG LIES) and big money have their own momentum which is very hard to impede. But that does not mean we should not stand up against them.

For many poorer African nations the choice is a simple one:

"Bullets" or "Food and Clean Water?"

Let us hope that in the future they may make the right choices for their people's sakes!

The United Nations has had multi-national forces in different hotspots as peace keepers. These include the Western Sahara, the Central African Republic, Mali, Haiti, Congo, Darfur in the Sudan and

Lebanon. UNIFIL is currently in Lebanon and has been requested to assist the Lebanese army to secure the Lebanon Syria border. The terrorist group Hezbollah want this border to remain uncontrolled so that it may cross at will along with terrorists and refugees. Currently there are 1.4 million Syrian refugees in Lebanon, a country of only 4 million. One can imagine the stress this has produced on both the government and the Lebanese people. Terrorist attacks on Christian minorities continue. It is to be noted that the UN does not participate with ground forces as peace keepers in Iraq, Syria or Afghanistan. These are left to US led coalitions. Nigeria and a few other African nations are also left to their own devices to combat terrorist groups. Also at present, Israel and Palestine have no UN peace keepers to assist with peace keeping operations on the ground in either state. Members of the United Nations Relief and Works Agency for Palestine Refugees are in Gaza doing good work. However, the situation of these two nations is often discussed in the Security Council and resolutions framed. Many majority Muslim nations such as Iran and even Indonesia still have an immature approach to Israel as a nation which further aggravates the situation especially when they make resolutions such as "Zionism is a form of racism". The 'land grab' from the Palestinians by Israel also presents an insurmountable hurdle that the UN has not yet dealt with severely enough! Thus murder and hatred continue.

Sovereign States and National Interests

We have recently seen the release of the Panama Papers where companies and individuals were listed disclosing their offshore investments thus avoiding substantial taxation on their wealth. International corporations are well known for employing the most astute accountants to find new ways to avoid taxation. One way is to place their head office in a poorer country where little tax is paid. Another tool for hiding wealth is in property investment. Central London along with the CBDs of most capital cities around the world offer opportunities for the very rich to hide their wealth. These tactics cheat the government and in turn the people of the nation by illegal decrements on the economy.

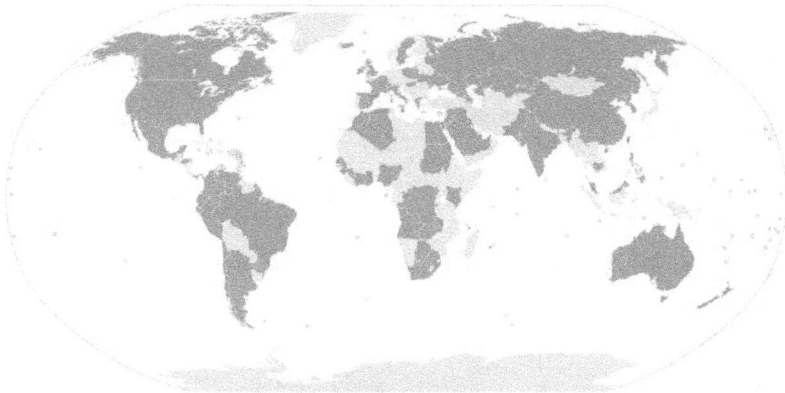

Countries with high profile persons implicated in the Mossack Fonseca papers (Panama Papers).

While offshore business entities are often not illegal, reporters found that some of the Mossack Fonseca shell corporations were used for illegal purposes, including fraud, kleptocracy*, tax evasion, and [*state in which those in power exploit national resources and steal; rule by a thief or thieves] evading international sanctions! More than 500 banks registered nearly 15,600 shell companies with Mossack Fonseca, with HSBC and its affiliates accounting for more than 2,300 of the total.

Foundations Firms Offshore Customers Through Banks:

Headquarters	Bank	Number of foundations
Luxembourg	Experta Corporate & Trust Services (100% subsidiary of BIL)	1659
Luxembourg	Banque J. Safra Sarasin – Luxembourg S.A.	963
Guernsey	Credit Suisse Channel Islands Limited	918
Monaco	HSBC Private Bank (Monaco) S.A.	778
Switzerland	HSBC Private Bank (Suisse) S.A.	733
Switzerland	UBS AG (subsidiary Rue du Rhône in Ginebra)	579
Jersey	Coutts & Co Trustees (Jersey) Limited	487
Luxembourg	Société Générale Bank & Trust Luxembourg	465
Luxembourg	Landsbanki Luxembourg S.A.	404
Guernsey	Rothschild Trust Guernsey Limited	378
Spain	Banco Santander	119
Spain	BBVA	19

The lame response to journalists by Mossack Fonseca was simply: "Our industry is not particularly well understood by the public!"... which in all fairness is true!

The unpalatable truth is that many high profile persons in governments or major corporations around the world have hidden investments stashed away in these havens beyond the reach of the taxman. The papers name them all!

However, the unfortunate truth regarding military hardware manufacturers is that they provide jobs and contribute greatly to a country's economy, especially those countries that have a long history of expertise in these products. But one might argue "is it in the long term national interest to be an exporter of serious weapons such as high explosives, bombs, missiles, naval ships and fighter aircraft?" Will, one day, the pigeons come home to roost i.e will all this armament production backfire on the nation?

Nations that produce arms and munitions then sell on to other nations have a daunting responsibility, particularly when the weapons are then used in a war. Weapons seized from the enemy forces in both Afghanistan and Syria were found to have originated across dozens of countries. Kalashnikov copies from China, small arms from India and a host of smaller European countries. Chemicals used to make poison gases found in Saddam Hussein's Iraq were sourced from major chemical companies operating in wealthy countries in central Europe. Semtex used by ISIL can also be traced back to European sources. [I stated in an earlier chapter that semtex, if produced by a recognised company, is seeded with a marker chemical that identifies its place of origin!]

It is ultimately the responsibility of the manufacturers to have control over who they sell their product to. The problem here is that old stock can be sold on to a third party and with the passage of time, difficult to point a finger and take legal action. Nations do employ inspectors that check inventory of producers of base chemicals as well as hardware used for war but they are not always reliable. If handgun makers were responsible, how is it that illegal shipments find their way to overseas nations? Looking back to the graphs on homicides per nation we see that many South American nations have incredibly high homicide rates such as Brazil, Venezuela, El Salvador etc. Many of these countries have their own gun manufacturers but not necessarily complex armament companies. But along with drugs, they have sufficient banditos and criminals involved in the export trade of handguns. Some of these are poor copies but others quite good copies of well known brands.

Nations such as Pakistan, China and North Korea are known to supply weapons via middle men to hot spots in the world where there is political instability and minor wars going on. Some countries like Australia, the UK and New Zealand have a tight rein over automatic weapons. One wonders how the terrorists in Belgium and France were able to get hold of Kalashnikovs and other fully automatic weapons to inflict extreme carnage on the innocent?

No doubt investigations asking these questions are ongoing. We, the public, don't always get to hear the answers!

But as countries less experienced in producing weapons and explosive materials continue with petty wars, in time, they soon become competent at bomb making, gun manufacture and more heavy armament making. This has been the legacy of all those European nations that, in recent history, were colonial powers throughout the world. Military expertise and procedural protocols have been spread. Former primitive nations have become mature technologically and in doing so have become sophisticated in training and equipping their armed forces. This then calls for much needed 'block cooperation' in the various regions of the world. ISIL, the Taliban and Boco Haram would soon disappear with more cooperation of the police and armed forces of neighbouring nations to where they act.

Current Known Terror Groups:

Abdullah Azzam Brigades

Al-Qaeda in Sinai Peninsula

Al-Qaeda in the Islamic Maghreb

Allied Democratic Forces

Ansar al-Sharia (Libya)

Ansar al-Sharia (Tunisia)

Ansar Bait al-Maqdis

Ansar Dine

Ansaru

Armed Islamic Group of Algeria

Al-Barakat

Boko Haram

Egyptian Islamic Jihad

Al-Gama'a al-Islamiyya

Al-Itihaad al-Islamiya

Jabhatul Islamiya

Libyan Islamic Fighting Group

Lord's Resistance Army

Moroccan Islamic Combatant Group

Al-Mourabitoun (militant group)

Movement for Oneness and Jihad in West Africa

Muaskar Anole

Mujahideen Shura Council in the Environs of Jerusalem

Muslim Brotherhood

Muslim Brotherhood in Egypt

Ras Kamboni Brigades

Al-Shabaab (militant group)

Soldiers of Egypt

Tunisian Combat Group

Almost all of the above are Islamic so I will note other non-Islamic terror groups below:

Fuerzas Armadas Revolucionarias De Colombia (FARC)

Revolutionary Armed Forces of Colombia

From 1964 this leftist guerrilla organization has been involved in the Colombian Civil War. FARC is the militant wing of the Colombian Communist Party. FARC claims to represent the poor people of rural Colombia and has around 7,000 to 10,000 active members including child soldiers. The group is notoriously known for using landmines and is held responsible for the death of 460 soldiers and thousands of civilians. FARC funds itself through illicit drug production and distribution, kidnap for ransom, illegal mining and extortion.

Revolutionary Struggle / Epanastatikos Agonas (EA)

EA is a Greek militant group that has been active since 2003. The group is infamous for their anarchist and anti-globalization views and are known for attacking government buildings, major banks, business institutions, police stations and the American embassy in Athens. They seek to bring a revolution in Greece.

Euskadi Ta Askatasuna (ETA)

Primarily operating in Spain and France ETA is a Basque nationalist and separatist organization founded in 1958 to promote Basque culture with the goal of establishing an independent Basqueland. ETA is accused of committing attacks on politicians, judges, journalists, businessmen, and tourists, killing over 829 people. The group's most well known dirty deed was the assassination of President Luis Carrero Blanco. ETA had also made assassination attempts on Prime Minister José María Aznar and King Juan Carlos. Over the years, owing to their notoriety, the group is said to have been losing sympathy of its supporters.

Shining Path / Sendero Luminoso

Shining Path is a communist guerrilla group in Peru formed in 1980. Their aim is to overthrow the Peruvian government and establish a Marxist government in its place. Though the group mainly draws its support from peasants they also often lead violent attacks on peasants whom they suspect of supporting the government. They therefore are responsible for carrying out numerous brutal massacres and running labour camps. There have been reported 31,000 deaths and disappearances related to Shining Path's conflict with the Peru government. But since the arrest of its leader Abimael Guzman in 1992, Shining Path has declined in its activities.

Real Irish Republican Army (RIRA)

An offshoot of the Irish Republican Army (IRA), RIRA's main goal was to unite Northern Ireland and the Republic of Ireland. Before RIRA's leaders were arrested in 2001, the groups had committed several terrorist activities in the UK and Republic of Ireland mainly targeting British military and the Northern Ireland police force. RIRA's most notorious work was the bombing of Omagh in 1998, killing 29 people and injuring 220 others making it the deadliest terrorist incident in Northern Ireland's history. This act came after the formal Peace Agreement which stands until today despite the tragedy!

Ulster Defense Association (UDA)

In Northern Ireland a loyalist militant organization was founded in 1971 with the objective of protecting Protestants from Catholics. UDA vehemently opposes uniting Northern Ireland with the Republic of Ireland and is responsible for 259 deaths, mostly Catholics. Also known as the Ulster Freedom Fighters (UFF) UDA's most recognised terrorist attack was the massacre of Greysteel, a predominantly Catholic village, in 1993. The UDA/UFF declared ceasefire in 1994 but continued violent attacks until a campaign for disarmament in 2007 officially ended it. Hopefully peace will endure and religious hatred will dissipate with time. It is the only sensible way forward!

New People's Army (NPA)

Formed in 1969 NPA is the Communist Party of the Philippines's armed wing. It operates in rural areas and commits heinous crimes. The group advocates left wing people's revolution ideology. The NPA has allegedly been involved in a prison raid, attacks on mining sites, attacks on the military, the police, and even government informers. They justify their actions saying they are in defence of the poor but NPA has a reputation of committing violence and extortion on the same poor people. In 1989, the NPA assassinated the US Army Colonel James "Nick" Rowe who was assisting a military program of the Philippine Army. Up until now, 40000 lives have been lost in the conflict between the NPA and government forces.

Aum Shinrikyo

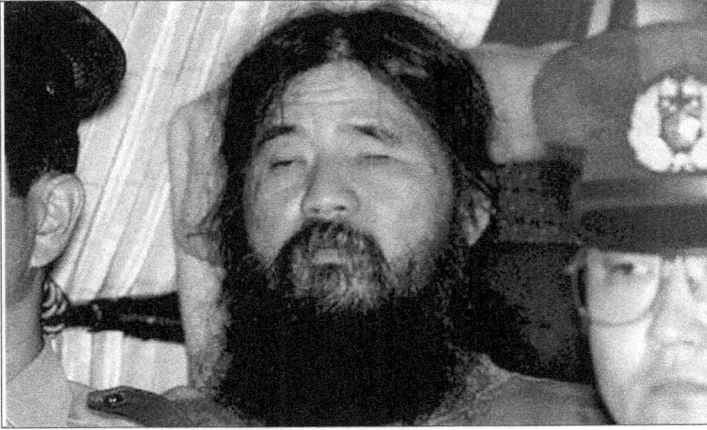

Aum Shinrikyo is a Japanese cult organisation established on the mixed philosophical beliefs of Christianity, yoga, Nostradamus' prophecies, and various conspiracy theories by Shoko Asahara in 1984. The terrorist group is known to carrying out brainwashing sessions on its members using electric shocks, LSD and other drugs. The group has around 40,000 worldwide members with 9,000 members residing in Japan. Aum Shinrikyo gained international prominence in 1995 with their sarin gas attack in the Tokyo subway system, killing 13 commuters and injuring several more. Their purpose was to bring about an apocalypse. In recent years there has been little interest in the group with no further attacks on the public. Hopefully they are a spent force!

Kahane Chai

An Israeli political party, Kach was founded by the infamous Meir Kahane in 1971. Following Kahane's assassination, Kahane Chai broke away from the main Kach fraction in 1991. It was a far right political party that advocated extreme Jewish supremacy and was responsible for spreading racism towards Arabs. The party had been accused of many notorious works like the bombing of a girls' school, conspiring and assassinations. The Kahane Chai had demonstrated open support for Baruch Goldstein – a Jewish man who killed 29 Palestinians in 1994 after which the party was finally banned by the Israeli government in the same year. Unfortunately sporadic killings of both Muslims and Jews continues in the Israel/Palestine state until the present. This hatred between religions has retarded social development of both parties which have been influenced by other third parties outside the borders.

Lord's Resistance Army (LRA)

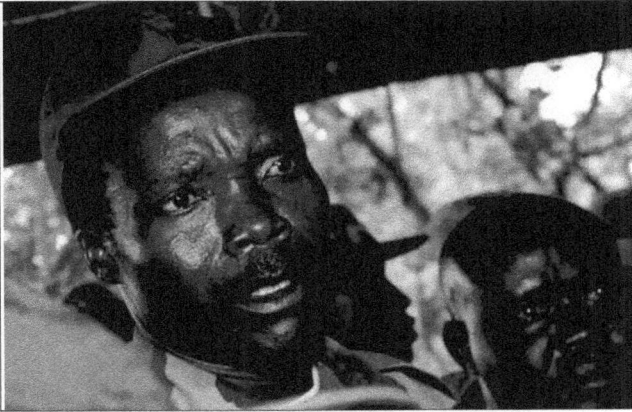

Founded in 1987, the LRA is a militant cult that operates in Uganda, South Sudan, the Democratic Republic of Congo, and the Central African Republic. Their self-proclaimed objective is to bring peace and prosperity in Uganda; however LRA is accused of widespread human rights violations including murder, abduction, mutilation, child sex slavery and making soldiers out of children. Between September 2008 and July 2011, the group had allegedly killed more than 2,300 people, abducted more than 3,000, and displaced over 400,000 across Central Africa.

Of course in America there has been quite a variety of flavours of terrorism some of which are reported below:

An FBI report shows that only a small percentage of terrorist attacks carried out on US soil between 1980 and 2005 were perpetrated by Muslims.

179

Princeton University's Loon Watch compiled the following chart from the FBI data:

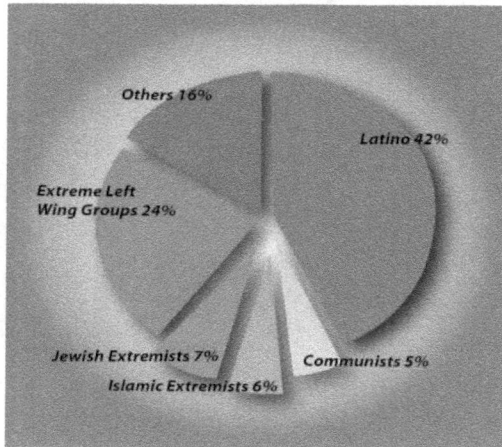

Terrorist Attacks on US Soil by Group, from 1980 to 2005, According to an FBI Database.

According to this data, there were slightly more Jewish acts of terrorism within the United States than Islamic (7% vs 6%). These radical Jews committed acts of terrorism in the name of their religion. These were not terrorists who happened to be Jews; rather, they were extremist Jews who committed acts of terrorism based on their religious passions, just like al Qaeda. (Loon Watch also notes that less than 1% of terror attacks in Europe were carried out by Muslims.)

US News and World Report noted in February of this year:

Of the more than 300 American deaths from political violence and mass shootings since 9/11, only 33 have come at the hands of Muslim-Americans, according to the Triangle Center on Terrorism and Homeland Security. The Muslim-American suspects or perpetrators in these or other attempted attacks fit no demographic profile- only 51 of more than 200 are of Arabic ethnicity. In 2012, all but one of the nine Muslim-American terrorism plots uncovered was halted in the early stages. That one, an attempted bombing of a Social Security office in Arizona, caused no casualties.

Mind you it does say 'since the 9/11 attack!' It must be remembered that in that attack:

> "The September 11 attacks killed 2996 people and injured more than 6000 others. These immediate deaths included 265 on the four planes, 2606 in the World Trade Center and in the surrounding area, and 125 at the Pentagon. The attacks of September 11, 2001, were the deadliest terrorist act in world history and the most devastating foreign attack on American soil since the sneak attack by the Japanese on Pearl Harbor on December 7, 1941."

Further, the data does not include the more recent terror attacks in San Bernardino and Orlando! [see appendix]

I have already outlined the most deadly attacks in Australia each of which had nothing to do with Islamic terrorism. Although the Lindt Café attack in Sydney was labelled such, most people believe that the perpetrator, Monis, was a nutter with serious psychological problems. The other deadly murder by a teenager in Sydney still has unanswered questions. The most pertinent is the fact that this boy was of Kurdish descent which begs the question "how was he radicalised?" It was claimed that his sister found her way to Syria and believed later to have been killed by a US drone attack.

Many of the recent acts of terrorism in the UK, France and other European countries were enacted by Muslims born in those countries albeit assisted by outsiders.

Combatants joining ISIL have flocked to Syria/Iraq from all corners of the globe. Prophecies in both the Bible and the al Koran point to a final battle on Earth in this part of the world but hopefully that will never eventuate.

We have seen then that sovereign nations all have their cultures, religions and politics which shape their identity and lead them to peace or confrontation with their neighbours. Religious terrorism and extremism, however, knows no geographical boundaries. Isolated bands of communists also still terrorise various countries. All of these groups require money and resources to continue their crusades... however they also need suppliers of weapons and military materials which, at present, are not so difficult to come by!

Warehouses and Silos

Silently they wait through night and day as ghosts beneath the grave. They have no thoughts or dreams but rest sleeping quietly and still until a spark stirs and ignites... then their destiny will be fulfilled and the whole Earth shall shake and millions will weep as they finally reach their targets.

Currently there are tensions between Russia and the West mainly due to Russia's involvement in the civil strife within the Ukraine and particularly its annexation of the Crimea. Added to this is its support for the al Assad regime in Syria and indiscriminate bombing of rebel held areas resulting in the deaths of hundreds of civilians.

Apart from forays between Russian and English soccer hooligans I see no possibility of any conflict between NATO forces and Russia based on a very simple premise: *there can be no winner!*

Both the West (in particular the US) and Russia have harboured thousand upon thousand of nuclear and thermonuclear weapons deep in silos, gathering dust and ticking away the decades waiting to be called upon in the event of some major conflict. A single thermonuclear weapon has the ability to vaporise a whole city the size of London or Moscow and leave a radioactive cloud that will wander hither and thither, willy nilly bringing more disease and destruction randomly over the ground it covers, possibly tens of thousands of square kilometres. The fearful thing is that there are generals on both sides that would use them!

Table 2015   Estimates of Nuclear Weapons:

Nation	Number of Nuclear Weapons
USA	7000+
Russia	7500+
China	450+
UK	40+
France	175+
India	40+
Pakistan	20+
Israel	50+
NthKorea	3+

These weapons were developed in the 1950s and 1960s and are basically a legacy of the 'cold war' when Russia was a more obvious communist threat. The problem in 2016 (and onwards) is that civil governments on all sides are unable to rid themselves of these harbingers of 'the end of human civilisation'. Is it not strange that the US, China and Russia have each spent trillions of dollars creating a system of mass destruction that cannot be used but also seemingly cannot be dismantled! Further, it costs billions per annum to maintain these systems in permanent readiness. I wish someone would explain to me the logic of this bizarre situation!

If the United Nations were indeed the United Nations without the inner club holding back, in many instances, its sole purpose of existence, it might enact laws where any nation holding a 'weapon of mass destruction' is fined a billion dollars per annum per weapon until they are all dismantled. I am certain that such huge sums of cash might be put to very good use in the poorer third world for basic commodities such as food and water. We might then move on to schools, hospitals, housing and the entire infrastructure to create healthy sustainable communities in all the nations! But you know, that fellah Tom Law is a bit of a dreamer! Presently the United States, as part of NATO, has hundreds of these weapons deployed in various parts of Western

Europe and Turkey. Seemingly, these are viewed as a deterrent against Russia in the improbable scenario of some limited war between NATO and the East. Do all the peoples of Europe feel comfortable with this situation? Tom Law suggests that ALL the nations on the planet demand that ALL these WMDs now be totally dismantled with the economic consequences spelled out for any refusal! To hell with the club!

Incidentally, some of the most powerful weapons have the equivalent explosive power of a mega tonne equivalent of TNT with dozens more in the 400 kilo tonne range! The Russians once had a 20 mega tonne bomb which has now been retired. The Chinese still maintain some 3.3 mega tonne bombs as part of their nuclear arsenal! Some estimates put Israel at more than 150 weapons now with India and Pakistan about 40 each. North Korea has a lot of hot air from King Jung's arse but possibly have 3 to 5 small weapons around 30 kilo tonne equivalent each.

But remember, the Hiroshima and Nagasaki bombs dropped in August 1945 were equivalent to about 15 kilo tonne and 20 kilo tonne TNT respectively!

See http://johnstonsarchive.net/nuclear for more information.

But placing the WMDs aside, there is still the horrific number of accumulated weapons that many nations have in reserve held in warehouses around the countryside of each. Added to this are those warehouses crammed tight with weapons and military materials owned by the manufacturers which they are hoping to sell off to other nations at those showy military fairs! I have discussed world expenditure on weapons in an earlier chapter and can only comment that the amounts of money are obscene, immoral and a stain on humanity in general. In the last couple of years we have seen war crimes committed by Saudi Arabia, Syria, Russia, Israel to name but a few. Accidental bombings of hospitals, schools and civilians have also occurred in Iraq and Afghanistan by the coalition partners. The manufacture and sale of armaments and military hardware perpetuate these crimes as well as the petty wars going on around the planet causing death, maiming and misery to millions of innocent people. A cynic might point out that profit is the root of all this evil where citizens in every country do not have the will to shackle their elected governments into expenditure on worthwhile things for the benefit of citizens rather than the huge and disproportionate amount spent on the military. Nice to hang medals on the wall of the lounge room awarded to a dead parent that fought in a war! I recall the famous folk song by Canadian singer Buffy Sainte-Marie: *'Universal Soldier'*…. by fighting… he thinks he'll put an end to war? Yes without the soldier there can be no conflict- a simple truth. But we are conned, governments and whole nations are conned. It has been a natural evolution from basic tribalism and survival that we must always *be prepared to kill.* And we need to do it in an ever more sophisticated way which necessitates higher expenditure! Technological advances give us more power to kill more efficiently but we need to stay ahead of perceived enemies. Career soldiers often cannot assist us with this argument as they need justification for what they have done. This reminds me of another famous folk song by Ralph McTell: *'Streets of London'*… the rain cries a little pity for one more forgotten hero and a world that doesn't care. Yes, when a particular battle is over people are

1 out of 4 Homeless MEN HAVE SERVED our COUNTRY in the military

186

not likely to dwell for long on the sacrifices and suffering and, disgracefully, our soldiers are oft neglected. I was amazed at the numbers of soldiers from old and recent wars that are homeless in the US (50000+), the UK (8000+) and even here in Australia (5000+). Proportionately, the Australian figures are the worst! It seems to be a very middle class thing to blame homelessness on the homeless- "… it's often their choice…" I have heard. I think it is a disgusting excuse. What they are really saying is: "… I'm alright Jack, in any case it is really not my problem!" We now see begging ads on TV asking for money to support some classes of veterans with specific post-service problems (see: soldieron.org.au).

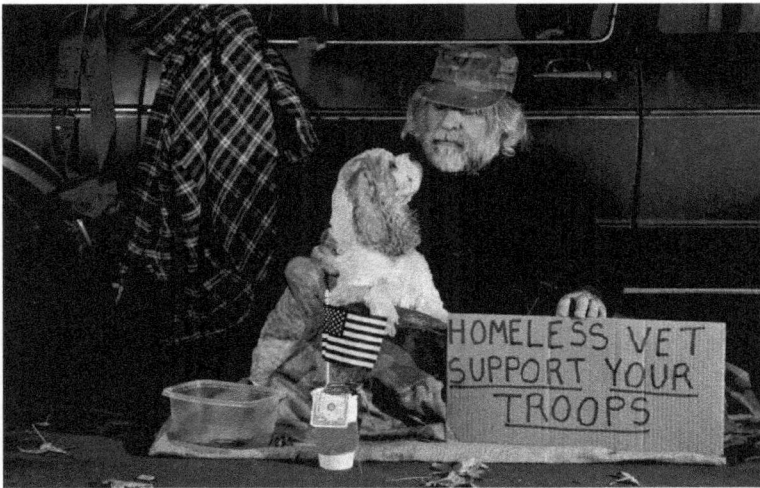

In many Western nations, apartments and homes are extremely expensive and may be overvalued by as much as 50%. Rents are also high and one wonders if the consumer price index (CPI) is properly calculated taking these into account. The pressure by foreign purchasers of properties in Melbourne and Sydney (particularly by the Chinese) certainly has pushed up prices making it extremely difficult for young families to achieve the dream of owning their own home. I believe the situation is similar in some major cities in the US, Canada and Britain. In fact wealthy foreign buyers have displaced many locals in central London with outrageously high prices having been paid. Much of the Monopoly board is foreign owned now!

Rental Trends – March quarter 2016

	Median weekly rent	Rent Index	Quarter % change	Annual % change
Melbourne	$390	214.7	1.2%	3.3%
Regional Victoria	$280	211.8	1.8%	2.3%
Victoria	$370	212.2	1.3%	3.2%

Notes

- (i) Median weekly rent is based on all new rental lettings for the quarter
- (ii) The Rent index is based on median rents stratified by location and dwelling type to control for compositional shifts in new lettings.
- (iii) Quarterly and Annual percentage change is calculated from the relevant Rent Indices, not median weekly rents.

[For further information please contact the Centre for Human Services Research and Evaluation at chsre@dhs.vic.gov.au]

Meanwhile, instead of solving this problem, governments continue to spend outrageous sums of money on military hardware for future defence even at the risk that by the time such hardware is in service, it is outmoded and past its use by date!

Manufacturers must get rid of their warehoused stock if they are to keep shareholders happy. The way to do this is to sell to other countries, sell to the black market and support certain wars as being righteous and justifiable.

Top nations of the world have become so interwoven and economically reliant on their home armaments and military hardware industries that governments too have little power over such vested interest. Their momentum and inertia is unstoppable as vast sums of money are to be made. They must also survive and continue to turn over profit at the expense of civilian casualties and wholesale destruction of cities and villages in war torn nations. But this carnage and havoc brings further problems to the global community in environmental degradation and the movement of millions of people as war refugees. This strain will bring its own unforeseeable consequences as well as enormous costs in reparations and rebuilding which must be borne by the peoples of wrecked countries. What a mess!

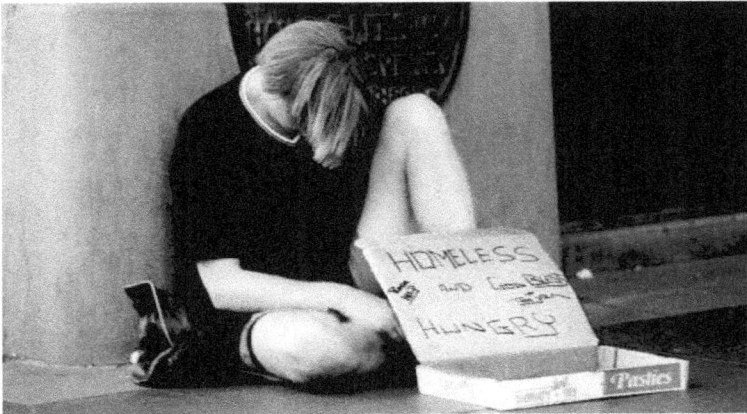

Referring to the Orlando massacre I personally have some very deep fears regarding the incident. As an analogy, you know, if you wish it to rain and you have science at your beg and call, one can hire a company to *'seed the clouds with chemicals'.*

Two events occurred in Orlando that weekend seemingly unrelated and only a few kilometres apart. The first was the murder of 22 year old singer Christina Grimmie, who made her name on NBC's *"The Voice."* She was signing autographs late Friday after a show at *The Plaza Live Theater* when a man approached and opened fire. She was rushed to a hospital, where she died. The shooter, 27, had two handguns, two additional loaded magazines and a large hunting knife according to police. He had travelled some 180 kilometre from his home town.

In the early hours of Sunday morning between 2 am and 5 am in *Orlando, Florida* an American-born man who allegedly pledged allegiance to ISIS gunned down 49 people early Sunday at a gay nightclub in Orlando, Pulse, becoming the deadliest mass shooting in the United States and the nation's worst terror attack since 9/11.

The gunman, Omar Mateen, 29, of Fort Pierce, Florida, had been interviewed by the FBI in 2013 and 2014 but was not found to be a threat. Mateen allegedly called 911 during the attack to pledge allegiance to ISIS. Orlando police shot and killed Mateen as he emerged with hostages about 5 am.

Mateen carried an assault rifle and a pistol (purchased legitimately from a gun shop just a few weeks before) into the packed Pulse club about 2 a.m Sunday and started shooting, killing 49 people and wounding a further 53. After a standoff of about three hours, while people trapped inside the club desperately called and messaged friends and relatives, police crashed into the building with an armoured vehicle and stun grenades and killed Mateen. Presidential nominee Trump was later to comment "if someone at the club was carrying a handgun, then pop pop… no more trouble, many people would have been saved!"

One is most disturbed at the calibre of this candidate, one desiring the highest political position in the land! Further, politicians in the senate blocked a resolution calling for tighter restrictions on checks on persons wanting to buy guns just a week or so later (June 2016). One wonders if the right persons are in political power in America and what Jo Blow in the street can do? Certainly protest and beg for the Senate to close for re-elections! It is not just the NRA that influences these senators, but the arms manufacturers and retailers. Checks need to be made on the assets and share-holdings of senators to determine who is in whose pocket!

A personal email to myself from a very brave and strong lady:

★Chellie PINGREE

Dear Mr Law   June 2016

Right now, my mom is sitting on the House floor with civil rights icon John Lewis and over 40 of her colleagues to force Paul Ryan and his NRA-backed Republicans to allow a vote on a common sense bill to prevent terrorists from buying guns.

But Republican leaders turned off the cameras to prevent the American people from seeing what's going on. They put the House in recess. And they're blocking any votes to protect innocent Americans from gun violence.

We must stand with my mom and demand Speaker Ryan and House Republicans to allow an up or down vote on common sense gun legislation. Tell Speaker Ryan and House Republicans: Allow a vote to keep guns out of the hands of terrorists and expand background checks now. Sign the petition!

Too many Americans have died from senseless gun violence, and Congress must act now to protect the American people. We urge you to allow an up or down vote on common sense gun legislation.

No one should ever fear for his or her life because terrorists or other criminals can get their hands on assault-style weapons with high-capacity magazines and walk into a public building with the goal of killing innocent Americans.

Congress has a responsibility to protect and defend the American people. A vote to keep guns out of the hands of terrorists and criminals will go a long way to do that.

Coincidentally at the time of the Orlando massacre, two candidates for the presidential election were in Florida. A Republican Party member was heard to say "I am falling behind... the people don't like me... I need something! For Christ's sake give me something!" It might be theorized that the first killing was a marker or indicator of things to follow. The mass killings were also committed by an 'out-of-towner', having travelled some 170 kilometre to his target.

Chemical psychology is an advanced technology in the 21st century. A person can be groomed to follow the will of another by an induced psychological mind implant. One can be hypnotized to perform any act against his/her natural predisposition... believe me! We live in a world where technological capability outstrips the ordinary person's concepts, understanding or inherent believability! In extreme politics, the means justifies the end. We have seen it before but not with such a level of sophistication. Of course, Tom Law is surmising on a possibility and has no concrete evidence other to comment that such scenarios are now possible. However, it is for this reason that I believe that *all* captured murderers and perpetrators of extreme massacres must be subjected to a blood test at the earliest opportunity to search for evidence of unfair play by a third party.

The British MP Jo Cox was shot and stabbed to death by an unlikely attacker, the 52 year old Tommy Mair. Again, this murder has the hallmark of a chemo-psychological behavioural implant to the perpetrator! It is well known that Mrs Cox got up the nose of the Russians over their complicity in war crimes against civilians in Syria. Also, the man was said to have had some connection to Nazi groups in both South Africa and the US. However, again I believe this man was groomed to perpetrate the crime. Tom Law is again speculating... but we live in a strange world in which (almost) anything is possible!

Incidentally, having little respect for Norway's sovereignty at present

whilst they are too civilised to enact the 'death penalty', I call on the British SAS to go there, apprehend, then execute the Nazi Anders Behring Breivik to show the world how such nefarious vermin should be treated. It is an affront to the 77 people he murdered (particularly in the light of his sentence being a mere 21 years) and all the courageous men and women that served and died in WWII, that he remains comfortably in prison! Best get rid of the rotten apple now before others join. This would be a more just punishment for the a/h !

You'd think that killing 77 constitutes an act of genocide!

[After all, we were there before in 1940 albeit for only 62 days at great cost whilst Vidkun Quisling was strutting around!]

Tom Law is prepared to go further than this:

Firstly let me define a modern day Nazi-

- One who likes to wear and parade the swastika symbol (with the exception of Hindus in Asia) as a badge or tattoo

- One who likes to wear and parade the 'death head' symbol as a badge, ring or tattoo (often  accompanied by the SS symbol)

- One who brazenly believes in 'white supremacy' and/or a master race

- One who regularly uses the Nazi 'Heil' salute in a serious and dedicated manner

- One who has intimidated, violently abused or murdered other humans on account of their race, religion or skin colour

- One that frequently harasses non-whites or anyone that opposes the ideologies of white supremacists
- One that belongs to a like-minded organisation and participates in pro-Nazi activities
- One that distributes any materials on any media that supports the ideologies of Nazism
- One that consistently is a 'Holocaust denier'
- One that consistently demonstrates that they are a 'Jew hater'

Anyone that scores 8 or more out of these 10 definitive points can be said to be a committed Nazi and Tom Law sees no reason why they should not have their 'breath taken away' and that such action be regarded as an 'act of war' and incur no punishment! But then that is me! We are currently experiencing a rise in the extreme right in a few European and Eastern European countries... let us hope that history is not going to repeat itself!

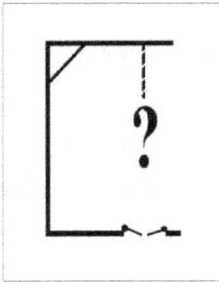

On the other hand, former South African Olympic athlete Oscar Pistorius should have been released from the charge of murdering his girlfriend (guilty or not) on the basis that his trial was essentially broadcast around the world to hundreds of millions of people. I even watched it in my remote location in Australia... how could that be labelled a fair trial?

In the appendices I have touched on other massacres in the US over the last few decades and I see no reason at all why similar acts will not continue for some time to come unless there is a radical turn around in the will of the people and the reaching to common sense by the politicians in power. The president cannot do all the work alone. Are the American people so easily swayed by sophisticated media hype tailored and tweaked to instil fear into their hearts? Fear of the bogey man, fear of the communist, fear of the Jew, fear of the Muslim, fear of the black man, fear of ghosts, and fear of a myriad of beasties and monsters conjured up by the controllers.

"If we don't have handguns in our handbags and houses, how will we protect ourselves from all the evil that is out to get us?"

From a distant perspective it is almost a childlike view of the world. And it is definitely not funny but more of a sad indictment to current society. The sentiment of 'keeping society safe' has reached an azimuth of madness. Sure, there will always be a small minority that wish to perform atrocities via hatred and a warped mind. But is it not better to remove the tools of trade presently so easy to acquire?

The Senate and various gun associations and clubs are doing a great injustice to the masses. It is not unreasonable for people to own a minimum of 'safe' firearms for sporting activities and I have never been against this. But handguns must be kept at club premises and limits must be placed on ownership. A new regime for owner registration of any firearm needs to be put in place (with a National Database) with stiff penalties for illegal sales i.e to unregistered persons. All weapons must carry clear identification and again, make it a serious offence for any alteration of a firearm. Private person to person sales must not eventuate. On the death of a gun owner, the state needs to enforce a compulsory buy-back scheme. Assault rifles and other military style weapons with rapid fire capability must remain illegal as far as the wider public are concerned.

A general amnesty and buy-back scheme is the way to go!

Without all these necessary things being put in place, the horrendous number of killings and maiming will continue and, as the heading says… "it will all end in tears!"

What the Individual Can and Must Do

Well at first you may throw your hands in the air and say "what can I do about things, I am just a single voice!"

But the author wishes to impress upon everyone that each and every voice of protest leads eventually to change! Many small drops make an ocean as somebody once said. Personally I find the everyday cop carrying a gun as both offensive and intimidating and I often get into a conversation asking why they feel it necessary to be armed.

In order to change gun laws and the way guns are readily available for sale, one has to be vigilant and petition politicians. In Australia we have made good progress, but the job is not finished yet. Certainly one should not vote for politicians that wish to relax the law. There are some very foolish statements and behaviours by right-leaning parties that should be placed last at the ballot box!

Further petitions on the number of guns any one person can hold are necessary. As stated over and over in this book I see no place for hand guns in the home... the club house safe is where they should be kept. Military style weapons must be forever banned and persons altering any firearm need to be punished under the law. National data bases are essential for maintenance of accurate information on registered persons and registered weapons. The sale of firearms must be strictly controlled with individuals not permitted to sell on their guns other than to registered retailers.

Protest against the giant military hardware manufacturers that are known to market and sell weapons to governments of poorer countries is both courageous and righteous! They should be placed at all times in the public view and their activities traced and trailed and advertised. Black market traders must be placed in prisons for very long periods as their crime is the worst! If your country's economy is propped up by the sale of armaments then I liken this to the sale of illicit drugs. Be not ashamed to disrobe the government and let the facts be laid bare for all to see and witness! We cannot make change for future generations without an expression of anger and disgust... but it can be done peacefully and intelligently! Exposure is distasteful to those in criminal or immoral activity. Their blustering red faces will exhale all sorts of excuses why they continue in their business. But these are the businesses of war, these are the profiteers making fistfuls of dollars and producing so much carnage and misery in the modern world. Perhaps I should use the word contemporary in place of modern because we have still a long way to go before bringing about a more utopian world society! Greed has always been the key motivation for doing the wrong thing, having the wrong mindset and throwing away one's conscience! Greed is predominantly the prime mover in the armaments business. And we all, as individuals, must fight against it with reason. Logic and reason are the weapons of choice to solve disputes between nations.

So here I am along two paths... firstly how to reduce gun related deaths within countries by exercising more stringent controls and secondly how to resolve the problem of the flow of more serious weapons to armies of poor countries and terrorist organisations. The first can be enacted by governments and their laws. The second can only be achieved by protest of people against the war-lord armament conglomerates and their middle men doing business around the world. Remember what I reiterate time and again:
"war and the weapons of war are now part of commerce deeply entrenched in the economies of many nations".

Only by the recognition of this fact by all the citizens of the world can we move forward and, if not totally eliminate wars, at least reduce the number of conflicts to the occasional skirmish that can be dealt with by the United Nations.

I have tried to point the way to achieve all these things. I am never embarrassed by being called a dreamer. I prefer to be labelled a visionary. Is not a healthy and safe life for the current poor in Africa, South America and Asia not a reasonable and sensible goal? To donate to charities to relieve the desperations of refugees and unlucky peoples in war regions of the globe is noble. But to conquer all we must get to the very nub and kernel and heart of the real problem... the spread of hideous and cruel weapons that destroy and remove what we expect as 'a normal life'. Normality to my mind includes:

- shelter over one's head of a good standard
- a caring and loving family
- a caring and sharing community
- availability of clean air and clean water
- a green and clean environment
- plentiful food
- a high standard of education facilities for children
- a high standard of hospitals and local health care facilities
- opportunities for meaningful employment and creativity for all
- a knowledge of the scientific method
- unhindered worship to God in one's own traditional way
- an acceptance of other cultures as well as pride in one's own
- sport as an outlet for the competitive spirit in humans
- an eye for waste and wrong direction in action

These are the basics that all humans deserve. War and expenditure on armaments and weapons in the modern age has created stolen generations in every country, stolen in the sense that they have been cheated of all the basics leading to happy and fruitful lives. All the nations are guilty to the highest degree! Democratic, communist, fascist... all have fallen far short of these ideals and tenets for their peoples. Inter-racial, inter-religious and other forms of hatreds have taken their toll. Governments have been all too ready to reach for the gun to solve human problems. With the channels of communication now available, is it not time to go down a new path and create truly sentient societies on this planet? I cannot see the point in venturing into space the way we are at present... other galactic civilisations will not welcome us. They will shun us as being too primitive and barbaric to bother with. Let us focus our energies on the proposals I have suggested above to satisfy the basic rights of all humans, wherever they abide. After all, it is not the fault of a child as to where he or she is born? All humans share the same rights and it is the responsibility of all humans to see that justice is done.

So what can you do as an individual? Continue to question everything and seek the best path for a rich, happy and meaningful life. But in doing so, try to avoid hurtful actions against others. Share these ideals with all you meet! Always give a portion of what you have to those with less but in a sensible way; you cannot give away all you have as then you take away your power to give! Be mindful of what is 'morally correct action' and what is detrimental action' in your life. Maintain a sense of community, dignity and respect. You are a child of this fantastic universe!

Lastly be careful to avoid extremes of politics and religion. None are absolute. All have human elements of imperfections within. We can always learn from others and acknowledge that humanity on this planet is diverse, as it should be. The greatest sin of all is to take another life, for human life is sacred. Those that take life offend God and indeed have no true religion other than a sickness of the mind. There is no reward in another place for this greatest of sins, only the void! Shun those that tell you otherwise!

Epilogue

This tome was to have been published at end February, 2016, some considerable time before the Orlando massacre, the Louisiana police shootings of young black men and the murder of police officers in Dallas, Texas. I would not use the word fortuitous; however these events have again brought the US nation to focus on the ongoing problem of 'too many guns' and 'the ease in which guns are obtainable' in America. It is unfortunate that the Orlando perpetrator was a Muslim especially following closely to the outpouring at the passing of Mohammad Ali, the famous boxer that did so much for Afro Americans. And one might observe that this incident fell comfortably into the lap of Donald Trump that has campaigned on the expulsion or at least to furnish a halt to further Muslim migration into America. I have already given an analysis on the sad episode with the recommendation that assault style weapons should not be available to the public and that a Federal database on gun ownership alongside similar databases on criminals and the insane or disturbed made available to authorities for cross checking.

But you know, no system will ever be perfect and it is nigh impossible to prevent a previously sane person from flipping to the dark side and committing a heinous crime of this magnitude. But the elimination of assault weapons and the prohibition of hand guns outside of club premises would certainly reduce the probability of these mass shooting events that have plagued American society for so long. Remove guns from the public then remove guns from the police! It may be that self-interest prevents senators from taking the correct action. But if it becomes the *will of the people*, then the senate must listen and act. Otherwise change will not come and the ongoing problem never addressed! The winners will continue to be the gun manufacturers and gun retailers. The losers will continue to be ordinary citizens.

I recently re-watched the movie '21 Jump Street' and wondered what value it expressed for young Americans? Yes, the theme was to rid a school of drug crime but the film in general displayed a decadent society where language had been reduced to primitive grunts and the police depicted as low caste morons. Gun violence was extreme and the humour more sad and pathetic than funny. The media also needs to take a long hard look at itself in this, the 21st century! America is capable of much more than this denigration of its people and culture!

I have suggested also in this book that ordinary day-to-day police not carry guns. This may be anathema to many police in both my country, Australia, and in the US. But there is wisdom in the proposed future scenario of a state where ordinary police do not carry side arms. Firstly, the temptation to shoot and ask questions later is eliminated. The chance of accidental murder is removed. The confidence of the public and the way it views and interacts with police is positively enhanced with an increase in respect for the service. As I have stated, personally I find an armed cop intimidating and, whilst cautious in her/his presence, cannot feel true respect for the officer. But if a citizen murders a member of the police force with neither rhyme nor reason, I would support the death penalty for the perpetrator. That is my stance, that is my value!

In the case of an extreme situation occurring where a senior officer, given the information, deems that a weapon is justified to prevent murder of innocent citizens (such as a terrorist attack or potential mass murder) then I believe that a specialist police force may be called into action. This needs to be a small but highly trained and professional body that can calm the situation or take necessary action to save or reduce the loss of life. And I do not see here the relevance of a quasi-military, over armed and aggressive bunch of trigger happy goons dying for 'a piece of the action' to place in their memoirs for the grand kids... no, that is the last thing one needs. We require intelligent handling of situations by a small professional group *with experience*! We have all too often seen a mental person on the street waving a knife being recklessly gunned down and killed where a wounding to disable the person might have been possible. Of course the logistics of this is not always assured where time is of the essence. In large centres such as cities, response time in getting specials to the scene is doable. However in more remote situations this can be problematic. The general thrust of my argument remains: a safer society is NOT one where there are guns everywhere, including those carried by police. I want to see the faces of the friendly cops that people can look up to and respect.

And I am not saying that policing is an easy job and my intent is not to castigate the force... far from it! It is a job that demands a myriad of skills in a modern society. I would be happy to see a more professional force that receives a considerably higher pay and one in which the training is longer and more comprehensive. I recently spoke with a young policeman from Queensland who had transferred to Victoria. I asked him why he had moved such a great distance interstate. His reply: "because you need a university degree to be a cop in Queensland!"

I assume he meant that the training is now both longer and more rigorous in that state. Well, that is how it should be!

The most tiresome bane and load that the police have to shoulder is anything to do with traffic and motorcars and their drivers. There must be other ways to alleviate this responsibility, particularly with regard to road offences such as speeding, drink driving etc. Having said this, dangerous criminals have been apprehended after being pulled over by the police implying a continual need for some policing of highways and byways. However a lot more could be done by unmanned machines that detect and report to a central computer for later action.

Domestic violence is also a very hard job for the police to become involved in and has proven to lead to most serious situations. Again, where the day-to-day cop finds herself or himself out of depth, specialist trained officers need to be called in. Where a serious crime has taken place in a domestic violence situation, I have repeatedly stated that a blood test for the perpetrator needs to be taken to add to evidence. Due to its prevalence in the community, crime researchers need data to build up any patterns to assist the community in general as a lead to try and reduce this type of crime.

Kitchen knives and items of furniture will always be there as potential weapons in the household. However there is no reason for handguns to be in the house. Somehow, this culture of fear (propagated by cheap rubbish TV programs and the weapons manufacturers) needs to change. A gun culture will always be dominated by fear. Fear of the thief, fear of the violent intruder, fear of the rapist or murderer, fear of the communist or Muslim hiding under the bed, fear of the family across the road because they are of a different colour or race. Such irrational behaviour needs to stop! The US has a long way to go. But as pointed out in an earlier chapter, homicides by guns are far greater in Latin American countries than in America and far fewer in Europe and

Australasia. American society needs to ask itself why and determine what sort of society it wants its children to grow up in in the future.

I have mentioned some of the arms manufacturers but the list is by no means comprehensive and fails to mention so many more in countries across the whole world. Few of these companies can be said to behave responsibly and morally when it comes to sales. Many are ready to bring their wares to expos to sell to foreign countries including the third world. Like some of our banking corporations that make most of their money from the debts of the poor, they prey on the third world and entice them with arms supplies and military hardware to make the various tin-pot dictatorships "look good" amongst their people! But it is these very nations that

(i)   don't really need all this stuff and more importantly

(ii)   cannot afford it!

Their tight economies should be distributed mainly in health and education infrastructures to build a better society. True wealth is in the accumulation of knowledge and skills in the cerebellum, not necessarily in material things alone.

Are small wars between poor nations artificially concocted by richer nations for their own monetary gain? It is a question! Is hatred between different ethnic groups, different religious schisms and different skin colours promulgated by the unseen hand of evil for the sake of profit and emptying warehouses full of products now obsolete to the rich nations? It is another question! Does this evil pervade the high tech advanced industrialised nations at the expense of the poorer and simpler? It is a question that must be asked and examined.

An overhaul of the United Nations is well overdue with the essential demise of the *'inner club'* bringing equality to the voices of all the nations. More than a 'pound of flesh' needs to be exacted from nations doing their worst to perpetuate the sales of armaments with gay abandon. Weapons of Mass Destruction must be evaporated now before any single despot is tempted to make use of them. A severe national penalty should be served as a sort of 'Corporation' punishment to bring about their demise. Monies paid in fines might go towards programs to end poverty and bring health and human dignity to those suffering under weak and uncaring regimes. Again I say:

"this can only come about by a complete restructuring of the United Nations, by removing the inner club and making it more democratic".

This inner club of the more powerful and wealthy nations also supports Private Security firms to protect its assets in poorer countries. As mentioned earlier, the connections of these companies to military hardware manufacturers poses an ever more complex problem where financial gain may overrule safe and smart behaviour. I see no need for many of these Private Security companies that seem, to my mind, to exacerbate some conflicts rather than solve them. Governments are too readily willing to submit to private armies- for that is what they are - to take the place of their own police forces and defence forces.

I have done all I can to paint a landscape of a future world where war, violence and particularly death or injury by firearms has been significantly reduced. My view and definition of a *'safe society'* is one in which citizens can go about their business free from *'fear'* during the daytime and during the night time. A society without firearms being carried anywhere by private citizens or by the state's law enforcers does not seem an unreasonable request. There remains a place for a limited number of firearms for recreational pursuits but under all the restrictions outlined. Not all will agree. However, I appeal to the sensible majority and beg that they are strong and resolute to make their voice heard and never yield until the job is done.

Some will argue forever that a nation needs to defend itself against a would-be aggressor. Further, that the individual also has the right to defend herself or himself against a would-be attacker. But I question both of these stances in an educated and smaller world where nations can use other means to settle differences and where a more powerful United Nations can place economic hardship on those that do not behave peacefully. The foisted 'culture of fear' must be examined and shown for what it really is: a mechanism for control and for monetary gain by the few over the majority. Names are to be named and fingers are to be pointed. Humanity has been given husbandry over all the earth, its lands, its seas and the air. Only by a restrained but combined effort can this continue so that the earth and all its diverse peoples can be cherished, nurtured and survive harmoniously. The methodology is not by 'rods of iron'… that epoch is at an end.

Reference Materials

Amnesty International: Arms Trade

Anderson, Casey; Horwitz, Joshua (2009). Guns, Democracy, and the Insurrectionist Idea. Ann Arbor, MI: University of Michigan Press.

Cornell, Saul (2006). A Well-Regulated Militia - The Founding Fathers and the Origins of Gun Control in America. New York, New York: Oxford University Press.

Barnett, Gary E. (June 24, 2008). Geo. J.L. & Sunstein, Cass (November 2008). "Comment: Second Amendment Minimalism: Heller vs Griswold" Harv. L. Rev.

The British Library – Defence Industry Guide (sources of information)

Campaign Against Arms Trade (UK)

CSIRO: Commonwealth Scientific & Industrial Research Organisation

ControlArms.org

Defense Industrial Base blog by Jeffrey Peter Bradford

FAS's Arms Sales Monitoring Project

The Guardian's arms trade report

Hemenway, David (2007). Private Guns, Public Health. University of Michigan Press.

Hersh, Seymore (2015). The Killing of Osama bin Laden

List of participators of the Defense System and Equipment international conference in London, 2003

Mulloy, D. (2004). American Extremism. Routledge.

SIPRI arms industry reports and database

SIPRI list of Top 100 arms-producing companies

SPADE Defense Index (NYSE: DXS) Defense sector market index

The True Cost of Global Arms Trade [infographic included]

Tushnet, Mark V. (2007). Out of Range: Why the Constitution Can't End the Battle Over Guns. Oxford University Press.

UN Office for Disarmament Affairs

US Arms Sales to the Third World from the Dean Peter Krogh Foreign Affairs Digital Archives

VICE NEWS
Australian Institute of Criminology: various reports

Viktor Bout arms trade case

Wikipedia, the free encyclopedia: Second Amendment to the United States Constitution

World Map and Chart of Arms exports per country by Lebanese-economy-forum, World Bank data

World Security Institute's Center for Defense Information

https://en.wikipedia.org/wiki/Arms_industry

http://www.cheatsheet.com/business/the-worlds-10-largest-arms-exporters.html/?a=viewall

http://www.theepochtimes.com

https://en.wikipedia.org/wiki/Port_Arthur_massacre_(Australia)

http://crimeresearch.org

http://www.ibisworld.com.au

https://www.dmoz.org

http://johnstonsarchive.net/nuclear

https://www.themonthly.com.au/issue/2014/may/1398866400/james-brown/guns-hire

http://www.securitydegreehub.com/30-most-powerful-private-security-companies-in-the-world/

Appendices

1.   *White House Executive Actions to Reduce Gun Violence*

Here are the details on how President Obama (2016) aims to improve background checks on gun buyers, community safety, mental health treatment and smart gun technology:

Summary:

- Expansion of Background Checks for private sales
- Bolster database of prohibited buyers
- Hiring of more background checkers and ATF agents
- Increase funding for mental health care
- Research and development of gun-safety technology

Press release by the White House on Executive actions on guns
Source: White House press release on Executive Actions to Reduce Gun Violence

The White House

Office of the Press Secretary
For Immediate Release
January 05, 2016

FACT SHEET: New Executive Actions to Reduce Gun Violence and Make Our Communities Safer

Gun violence has taken a heartbreaking toll on too many communities across the country. Over the past decade in America, more than 100,000 people have been killed as a result of gun violence and millions more have been the victim of assaults, robberies, and other crimes involving a gun. Many of these crimes were committed by people who never should have been able to purchase a gun in the first place. Over the same period, hundreds of thousands of other people in our communities committed suicide with a gun and nearly half a million people suffered other gun injuries. Hundreds of law enforcement officers have been shot to death protecting their communities. And too many children are killed or injured by firearms every year, often by accident. The vast majority of Americans (including the vast majority of gun owners) believe we must take sensible steps to address these horrible tragedies.

The President and Vice President are committed to using every tool at the Administration's disposal to reduce gun violence. Some of the gaps in our country's gun laws can only be fixed through legislation, which is why the President continues to call on Congress to pass the kind of commonsense gun safety reforms supported by a majority of the American people. And while Congress has repeatedly failed to take action and pass laws that would expand background checks and reduce gun violence, today, building on the significant steps that have already been taken over the past several years, the Administration is announcing a series of commonsense executive actions designed to:

1.   **Keep guns out of the wrong hands through background checks.**

- The Bureau of Alcohol, Tobacco, Firearms and Explosives (ATF) is making clear that it doesn't matter where you conduct your business- from a store, at gun shows, or over the Internet: If you're in the business of selling firearms, you must get a license and conduct background checks.

- ATF is finalizing a rule to require background checks for people trying to buy some of the most dangerous weapons and other items through a trust, corporation, or other legal entity.

- Attorney General Loretta E. Lynch has sent a letter to States highlighting the importance of receiving complete criminal history records and criminal dispositions, information on persons disqualified because of a mental illness, and qualifying crimes of domestic violence.

- The Federal Bureau of Investigation (FBI) is overhauling the background check system to make it more effective and efficient. The envisioned improvements include processing background checks 24 hours a day, 7 days a week, and improving notification of local authorities when certain prohibited persons unlawfully attempt to buy a gun. The FBI will hire more than 230 additional examiners and other staff to help process these background checks.

2.   **Make our communities safer from gun violence.**

- The Attorney General convened a call with US Attorneys around the country to direct federal prosecutors to continue to focus on smart and effective enforcement of our gun laws.

- The President's FY2017 budget will include funding for 200 new ATF agents and investigators to help enforce our gun laws.

- ATF has established an Internet Investigation Center to track illegal online firearms trafficking and is dedicating $4 million and additional personnel to enhance the National Integrated Ballistics Information Network.

- ATF is finalizing a rule to ensure that dealers who ship firearms notify law enforcement if their guns are lost or stolen in transit.

- The Attorney General issued a memo encouraging every US Attorney's Office to renew domestic violence outreach efforts.

3.   **Increase mental health treatment and reporting to the background check system.**

- The Administration is proposing a new $500 million investment to increase access to mental health care.

- The Social Security Administration has indicated that it will begin the rulemaking process to include information in the background check system about beneficiaries who are prohibited from possessing a firearm for mental health reasons.

- The Department of Health and Human Services is finalizing a rule to remove unnecessary legal barriers preventing States from reporting relevant information about people prohibited from possessing a gun for specific mental health reasons.

4.   **Shape the future of gun safety technology.**

- The President has directed the Departments of Defense, Justice, and Homeland Security to conduct or sponsor research into gun safety technology.
- The President has also directed the departments to review the availability of smart gun technology on a regular basis, and to explore potential ways to further its use and development to more broadly improve gun safety.

Congress should support the President's request for resources for 200 new ATF agents and investigators to help enforce our gun laws, as well as a new $500 million investment to address mental health issues.

Because we all must do our part to keep our communities safe, the Administration is also calling on States and local governments to do all they can to keep guns out of the wrong hands and reduce gun violence. It is also calling on private-sector leaders to follow the lead of other businesses that have taken voluntary steps to make it harder for dangerous individuals to get their hands on a gun. In the coming weeks, the Administration will engage with manufacturers, retailers, and other private-sector leaders to explore what more they can do.

New Actions by the Federal Government

Keeping Guns Out of the Wrong Hands through Background Checks

The most important thing we can do to prevent gun violence is to make sure those who would commit violent acts cannot get a firearm in the first place. The National Instant Criminal Background Check System (NICS), which was created by Congress to prevent guns from being sold to prohibited individuals, is a critical tool in achieving that goal. According to the Bureau of Justice Statistics, the background check system has prevented more than 2 million guns from getting into the wrong hands. We know that making the system more efficient, and ensuring that it has all appropriate records about prohibited purchasers, will help enhance public safety. Today, the Administration is announcing the following executive actions to ensure that all gun dealers are licensed and run background checks, and to strengthen the background check system itself:

- **Clarify that it doesn't matter where you conduct your business- from a store, at gun shows, or over the Internet: If you're in the business of selling firearms, you must get a license and conduct background checks.** Background checks have been shown to keep guns out of the wrong hands, but too many gun sales- particularly online and at gun shows- occur without basic background checks. Today, the Administration took action to ensure that anyone who is "engaged in the business" of selling firearms is licensed and conducts background checks on their customers. Consistent with court rulings on this issue, the Bureau of Alcohol,

Tobacco, Firearms and Explosives (ATF) has clarified the following principles:

- A person can be engaged in the business of dealing in firearms regardless of the location in which firearm transactions are conducted. For example, a person can be engaged in the business of dealing in firearms even if the person only conducts firearm transactions at gun shows or through the Internet. Those engaged in the business of dealing in firearms who utilize the Internet or other technologies must obtain a license, just as a dealer whose business is run out of a traditional brick-and-mortar store.

- Quantity and frequency of sales are relevant indicators. There is no specific threshold number of firearms purchased or sold that triggers the licensure requirement. But it is important to note that even a few transactions, when combined with other evidence, can be sufficient to establish that a person is "engaged in the business." For example, courts have upheld convictions for dealing without a license when as few as two firearms were sold or when only one or two transactions took place, when other factors also were present.

- There are criminal penalties for failing to comply with these requirements. A person who wilfully engages in the business of dealing in firearms without the required license is subject to criminal prosecution and can be sentenced up to five years in prison and fined up to $250,000. Dealers are also subject to penalties for failing to conduct background checks before completing a sale.

- **Require background checks for people trying to buy some of the most dangerous weapons and other items through a trust or corporation.** The National Firearms Act imposes restrictions on sales of some of the most dangerous weapons, such as machine guns and sawed-off shotguns. But because of outdated regulations, individuals have been able to avoid the background check requirement by applying to acquire these firearms and other items through trusts, corporations, and other legal entities. In fact, the number of these applications has increased significantly over the years- from fewer than 900 applications in the year 2000 to more than 90,000 applications in 2014. ATF is finalizing a rule that makes clear that people will no longer be able to avoid background checks by buying NFA guns and other items through a trust or corporation.

- **Ensure States are providing records to the background check system, and work cooperatively with jurisdictions to improve reporting.** Congress has prohibited specific categories of people from buying guns- from convicted felons to users of illegal drugs to individuals convicted of misdemeanor crimes of domestic violence. In the wake of the shootings at Virginia Tech in 2007, Congress also created incentives for States to make as many relevant records as possible accessible to NICS. Over the past three years, States have increased the number of records they make accessible by nearly 70 percent. To further encourage this reporting, the Attorney General has written a letter to States highlighting the importance of receiving complete criminal history records and criminal dispositions, information on persons disqualified for mental health reasons, and qualifying crimes of domestic

219

violence. The Administration will begin a new dialogue with States to ensure the background check system is as robust as possible, which is a public safety imperative.

- **Make the background check system more efficient and effective.** In 2015, NICS received more than 22.2 million background check requests, an average of more than 63,000 per day. By law, a gun dealer can complete a sale to a customer if the background check comes back clean or has taken more than three days to complete. But features of the current system, which was built in the 1990s, are outdated. The Federal Bureau of Investigation (FBI) will take the following steps to ensure NICS operates more efficiently and effectively to keep guns out of the wrong hands:

- FBI will hire more than 230 additional NICS examiners and other staff members to assist with processing mandatory background checks. This new hiring will begin immediately and increase the existing workforce by 50 percent. This will reduce the strain on the NICS system and improve its ability to identify dangerous people who are prohibited from buying a gun before the transfer of a firearm is completed.

- FBI has partnered with the US Digital Service (USDS) to modernize NICS. Although NICS has been routinely upgraded since its launch in 1998, the FBI is committed to making the system more efficient and effective, so that as many background checks as possible are fully processed within the three-day period before a dealer can legally sell a gun even if a background check is not complete. The improvements envisioned by FBI and USDS include processing background checks 24 hours a day, 7 days a week

220

to improve overall response time and improving notification of local authorities when certain prohibited persons unlawfully attempt to purchase a firearm.

Making Our Communities Safer from Gun Violence

In order to improve public safety, we need to do more to ensure smart and effective enforcement of our gun laws and make sure that criminals and other prohibited persons cannot get their hands on lost or stolen weapons. The Administration is therefore taking the following actions:

- **Ensure smart and effective enforcement of our gun laws.** In a call earlier today, the Attorney General discussed the importance of today's announcements and directed the Nation's 93 US Attorneys across the country to continue to focus their resources- as they have for the past several years under the Department's Smart on Crime initiative- on the most impactful cases, including those targeting violent offenders, illegal firearms traffickers, and dangerous individuals who bypass the background check system to acquire weapons illegally. During the call, the Attorney General also emphasized ongoing initiatives to assist communities in combating violent crime, including ATF's efforts to target the "worst of the worst" gun crimes. These efforts will also complement the following actions announced today:

- The President's budget for FY2017 will include funding for 200 new ATF agents and investigators who can help enforce our gun laws, including the measures announced today. Strategic and impactful enforcement will help take violent criminals off the street, deter other unlawful activity, and prevent guns from getting into the wrong hands.

- ATF is dedicating $4 million and additional personnel to enhance the National Integrated Ballistics Information Network (NIBIN). The NIBIN database includes ballistic evidence that can be used by analysts and investigators to link violent crimes across jurisdictions and to track down shooters who prey on our communities. In February 2016, ATF is standing up the National NIBIN Correlation and Training Center- which will ultimately provide NIBIN matching services at one national location, rather than requiring local police departments to do that work themselves. The Center will provide consistent and capable correlation services, making connections between ballistic crime scene evidence and crime guns locally, regionally, and nationally. These enhancements will support ATF's crime gun intelligence and enforcement efforts, particularly in communities most affected by violent crime.

- ATF has established an Internet Investigations Center (IIC) staffed with federal agents, legal counsel, and investigators to track illegal online firearms trafficking and to provide actionable intelligence to agents in the field. The IIC has already identified a number of significant traffickers operating over the Internet. This work has led to prosecutions against individuals or groups using the "dark net" to traffic guns to criminals or attempting to buy firearms illegally online.

- **Ensure that dealers notify law enforcement about the theft or loss of their guns.** Under current law, federal firearms dealers and other licensees must report when a gun from their

222

inventory has been lost or stolen. The regulations are ambiguous, however, about who has this responsibility when a gun is lost or stolen in transit. Many lost and stolen guns end up being used in crimes. Over the past five years, an average of 1,333 guns recovered in criminal investigations each year were traced back to a licensee that claimed it never received the gun even though it was never reported lost or stolen either. Today, ATF issued a final rule clarifying that the licensee shipping a gun is responsible for notifying law enforcement upon discovery that it was lost or stolen in transit.

- **Issue a memo directing every US Attorney's Office to renew domestic violence outreach efforts.** In the event of an emergency, victims of domestic violence should call 911 or otherwise contact state or local law enforcement officials, who have a broader range of options for responding to these crimes. To provide an additional resource for state, local, and tribal law enforcement and community groups focused on domestic violence, the Attorney General is issuing a memo directing US Attorney's Offices around the country to engage in renewed efforts to coordinate with these groups to help combat domestic violence and to prevent prohibited persons from obtaining firearms.

Increase Mental Health Treatment and Reporting to the Background Check System

The Administration is committed to improving care for Americans experiencing mental health issues. In the last seven years, our country has made extraordinary progress in expanding mental health coverage for millions of Americans. This includes the Affordable Care Act's end to insurance company discrimination based on pre-existing conditions, required coverage of mental health and substance use disorder services in the individual and small group markets, and an expansion of mental health and substance use disorder parity policies, all of which are estimated to help more than 60 million Americans. About 13.5 million more Americans have gained Medicaid coverage since October 2013, significantly improving access to mental health care. And thanks to more than $100 million in funding from the Affordable Care Act, community health centers have expanded behavioral health services for nearly 900,000 people nationwide over the past two years. We must continue to remove the stigma around mental illness and its treatment- and make sure that these individuals and their families know they are not alone. While individuals with mental illness are more likely to be victims of violence than perpetrators, incidents of violence continue to highlight a crisis in America's mental health system. In addition to helping people get the treatment they need, we must make sure we keep guns out of the hands of those who are prohibited by law from having them. Today, the Administration is announcing the following steps to help achieve these goals:

- **Dedicate significant new resources to increase access to mental health care.** Despite our recent significant gains, less than half of children and adults with diagnosable mental health problems receive the treatment they need. To address this, the Administration is proposing a new $500 million investment to help engage individuals with serious mental illness in care, improve access to care by increasing service capacity and the behavioral health workforce, and ensure that behavioral health care systems work for everyone. This effort would increase access to mental health services to protect the health of children and communities, prevent suicide, and promote mental health as a top priority.

- **Include information from the Social Security Administration in the background check system about beneficiaries who are prohibited from possessing a firearm.** Current law prohibits individuals from buying a gun if, because of a mental health issue, they are either a danger to themselves or others or are unable to manage their own affairs. The Social Security Administration (SSA) has indicated that it will begin the rulemaking process to ensure that appropriate information in its records is reported to NICS. The reporting that SSA, in consultation with the Department of Justice, is expected to require will cover appropriate records of the approximately 75,000 people each year who have a documented mental health issue, receive disability benefits, and are unable to manage those benefits because of their mental impairment, or who have been found by a state or federal court to be legally incompetent. The rulemaking will also provide a mechanism for people to seek relief from the federal prohibition on possessing a firearm for reasons related to mental health.

- **Remove unnecessary legal barriers preventing States from reporting relevant information to the background check system.** Although States generally report criminal history information to NICS, many continue to report little information about individuals who are prohibited by Federal law from possessing or receiving a gun for specific mental health reasons. Some State officials raised concerns about whether such reporting would be precluded by the Privacy Rule issued under the Health Insurance Portability and Accountability Act of 1996 (HIPAA). Today, the Department of Health and Human Services issued a final rule expressly permitting certain HIPAA covered entities to provide to the NICS limited demographic and other necessary information about these individuals.

Shaping the Future of Gun Safety Technology

Tens of thousands of people are injured or killed by firearms every year- in many cases by guns that were sold legally but then stolen, misused, or discharged accidentally. Developing and promoting technology that would help prevent these tragedies is an urgent priority. America has done this in many other areas- from making cars safer to improving the tablets and phones we use every day. We know that researchers and engineers are already exploring ideas for improving gun safety and the tracing of lost or stolen guns. Millions of dollars have already been invested to support research into concepts that range from fingerprint scanners to radio-frequency identification to microstamping technology.

As the single largest purchaser of firearms in the country, the Federal Government has a unique opportunity to advance this research and ensure that smart gun technology becomes a reality- and it is possible to do so in a way that makes the public safer and is consistent with the Second Amendment. Today, the President is taking action to further this work in the following way:

- **Issue a Presidential Memorandum directing the Department of Defense, Department of Justice, and Department of Homeland Security to take two important steps to promote smart gun technology.**

- Increase research and development efforts. The Presidential Memorandum directs the departments to conduct or sponsor research into gun safety technology that would reduce the frequency of accidental discharge or unauthorized use of firearms, and improve the tracing of lost or stolen guns. Within 90 days, these agencies must prepare a report outlining a research-and-development strategy designed to expedite the real-world deployment of such technology for use in practice.

- Promote the use and acquisition of new technology. The Presidential Memorandum also directs the departments to review the availability of smart gun technology on a regular basis, and to explore potential ways to further its use and development to more broadly improve gun safety. In connection with these efforts, the departments will consult with other agencies that acquire firearms and take appropriate steps to consider whether including such technology in specifications for acquisition of firearms would be consistent with operational needs.

2.   *Categories of Firearms in Australia*

The National Firearm Agreement defines categories of firearms, with different levels of control for each, as follows:.

- **Category A**: Rimfire rifles (not semi-automatic), circuit loaded firearms. shotguns (not pump-action or semi-automatic), air rifles including semi automatic, and paintball gun. A "Genuine Reason" must be provided for a Category A firearm.
- **Category B**: Centrefire rifles including bolt action pump action, circuit loaded and lever action (not semi-automatic), muzzleloading firearms made after 1 January 1901.
- **Category C**: Pump-action or self-loading shotguns having a magazine capacity of 5 or fewer rounds and semi automatic rimfire rifles. Primary producers, farm workers, firearm dealers, firearm safety officers, collectors and clay target shooters can own functional Category C firearms.
- **Category D**: Self-loading centrefire rifles, pump-action or self-loading shotguns have a magazine capacity of more than 5 rounds. Functional Category D firearms are restricted to government agencies, occupational shooters and primary producers in some states. Collectors may own deactivated Category D firearms.
- **Category H**: Handguns including air pistols and deactivated handguns. Neither South Australia nor Western Australia requires deactivated handguns to be regarded as handguns after deactivation. This situation prompted the deactivation and diversion of thousands of handguns to the black market in Queensland- the loophole shut since 2001) This class is

available to target shooters and certain security guards whose job requires possession of a firearm. To be eligible for a Category H firearm, a target shooter must serve a probationary period of 6 months using club handguns, after which they may apply for a permit. A minimum number of matches yearly to retain each category of handgun and be a paid-up member of an approved pistol club. Target shooters are limited to handguns of .38 or 9mm calibre or less and magazines may hold a maximum of 10 rounds. Participants in certain "approved" pistol competitions may acquire handguns up to .45", currently Single Action Shooting and Metallic Silhouette. IPSC shooting is approved for 9mm/.38/.357 sig, handguns that meet the IPSC rules, larger calibres such as .45 were approved for IPSC handgun shooting contests in Australia in 2014. Barrels must be at least 100mm (3.94") long for revolvers, and 120mm (4.72") for semi-automatic pistols unless the pistols are clearly ISSF target pistols; magazines are restricted to 10 rounds.

- **Category R/E**: Restricted weapons, such as machine guns, rocket launchers, full automatic self loading rifles, flame-throwers, anti-tank guns, howitzers and other artillery weapons can be owned by collectors in some states provided that these weapons have been rendered permanently inoperable. They are subject to the same storage and licensing requirements as fully functioning firearms.

Certain antique firearms (generally muzzle loading black powder flintlock firearms manufactured before 1 January 1901) can in some states be legally held without a licence. In

229

other states they are subject to the same requirements as modern firearms. All single-shot muzzle loading firearms manufactured before 1 January 1901 are considered antique firearms. Four states require licences for antique percussion revolvers and cartridge repeating firearms, but in Queensland and Victoria a person may possess such a firearm without a licence, so long as the firearm is registered (percussion revolvers require a licence in Victoria).

Organisations

The largest organisation of firearms owners is the Sporting Shooters Association of Australia, with 175,000 members (2015 figures) SSAA state branches are responsible for lobbying on local issues, while SSAA National addresses Federal legislation and international issues. SSAA National has non-government organisation (NGO) status at the United Nations and is a founding member of The World Forum on the Future of Sport Shooting Activities (WFSA), which also has NGO status. SSAA National has a number of people working in research and lobbying roles. In 2008, they appointed journalist and media manager Tim Bannister as Federal Parliamentary lobbyist.

For handguns, one major organisation in Australia is Pistol Australia.

There are several other national bodies, such as Field and Game Australia, the National Rifle Association of Australia, the International Practical Shooting Confederation (IPSC), the Australian Clay Target Association and Target Rifle Australia. These national bodies with their state counterparts concentrate on a range of sporting and political issues ranging from Olympic type competition through to conservation activities.

3. *Massacres in Australia*

Hoddle Street Massacre

The Hoddle Street massacre was a mass shooting that occurred on the evening of Sunday, 9 August 1987, in Hoddle Street, Clifton Hill, a suburb of Melbourne, Victoria, in Australia.

Perpetrator: Julian Knight

Start date: August 9, 1987

Deaths: 7

Attack types: Mass murder, Massacre

Port Arthur Massacre

The Port Arthur massacre of 28–29 April 1996 was a killing spree in which 35 people were killed and 23 wounded. It occurred mainly at the historic Port Arthur former prison colony, a popular tourist site in south-eastern Tasmania, Australia.

Perpetrator: Martin Bryant

Start date: April 28, 1996

Deaths: 35

Attack types: Mass murder, Carjacking, Arson

Strathfield Massacre

The Strathfield massacre was a shooting rampage in Strathfield, Sydney, Australia, on 17 August 1991. The shooter was Wade Frankum, who killed himself as police arrived at the scene. The incident left eight dead and six wounded.

Start date: August 17, 1991

Deaths: 8   Injured: 6

Attack types: Spree killer, Massacre, Murder-suicide

Queen Street Massacre

The Queen Street massacre was a spree-killing that occurred on 8 December 1987 at the Australia Post offices at 191 Queen Street in Melbourne, Victoria. The attack resulted in nine fatalities, including the perpetrator, and five injuries.

Start date: December 8, 1987

Weapon: M1 carbine

Deaths: 9   Injuries: 5

Attack types: Mass murder, Murder-suicide

The Russell Street Bombing

This refers to the 27 March 1986 bombing of the Russell Street Police Headquarters complex in Russell Street, Melbourne, Victoria, Australia.

Start date: March 27, 1986

Attack type: Car bomb

Perpetrators: Craig Minogue, Stan Taylor

Deaths: 1 (a policewoman)   Injured: 22

Belanglo State Forest Murders, NSW

The backpacker murders were a spate of serial killings that took place in New South Wales, Australia, during the 1990s by various methods including shootings.

Dates: 1989–1993

Weapons: axes, knives and guns

Attack types: Murder

Perpetrator: Ivan Robert Marko Milat

Deaths: between 7 and 12, possibly more

Also, possible shooting of a taxi cab driver in 1962

The author thinks it a pity that we are "so civilised", in fact "too civilised", to exact justice against all of the above perpetrators of such heinous crimes! I encourage all my readers to particularly read the report on all the events of the day of the Port Arthur Massacre then ask yourself the obvious question!

https://en.wikipedia.org/wiki/Port_Arthur_massacre_(Australia)

Mass Killings of Australians Outside of Australia:

Oct 2002, Kuta, Bali, Indonesia. 202 killed (88 Australian, 38 Indonesian, 27 UK, 7 US and representatives of 20 other nationalities), 209 injured in Paddy's Bar and the Sari nightclub. Car bomb of potassium chlorate and suicide back pack carried out by al Qaeda affiliates Jemmah Islamiyah. Imam Samudra, Amrozi Nurhasyim and Ali Ghufron were executed by firing squad in 2008.

Sep 2004 Australian Embassy* bombing, Jakarta, Indonesia. Car bomb killing 9 and injuring 150, all Indonesians. Perpetrated by Jemmah Islamiyah.

*Actually, no Australians died in this event!

Oct 2005 2nd Bali bombings at Jimbaran and Beach Resort, South Bali, Indonesia. 20 killed (15 Indonesians, 4 Australians and 1

234

Japanese) plus 129 injured (mostly Indonesian). Additionally killed were the three suicide bombers belonging to Jemmah Islamiyah.

July 2009 JW Marriott and Ritz-Carlton Hotels in Jakarta, Indonesia, were hit by simultaneous bombings caused by suicide terrorists belonging to Jemmah Islamiyah and al Qaeda. 9 died (including 3 Australians) and 53 injured (a handful of foreigners but mostly Indonesians).

July 2014 Malaysian Flight MH17 over the Ukraine Near Hrabove, Donetsk Oblast. Flying from Amsterdam to Kuala Lumpur. Killed all 298 on board including 193 Dutch, 43 Malaysian, 27 Australian, 12 Indonesian and other nationalities. Cause: surface to air missile from a mobile Soviet-designed Buk missile system fired by pro-Russian separatists. However, this has been constantly denied by Russian authorities.

2002-2015 Afghanistan ADF personnel: 41 killed, 264 wounded

2012-2015 Australians killed in Iraq fighting IS(with Kurds):3

2012-2015 Australians killed in Syria/Iraq fighting with IS: >50 (estimate) of approximately 165 that have joined

2003-2015 Overseas Private Security Firms: killed 6

4.   *Massacres in the United States of America*

Below are listed some of the more serious massacres in America in recent years. The list is not comprehensive:

Howard Unruh, a World War II veteran, shot and killed 13 of his neighbors in Camden, New Jersey, in 1949. Unruh barricaded himself in his house after the shooting. Police overpowered him the next day. He was ruled criminally insane and committed to a state mental institution.

Austin, University of Texas- Charles Joseph Whitman opened fire from the school's tower, killing 16 people and wounding 30 in 1966. Police officers shot and killed Whitman, who had killed his mother and wife earlier in the day.

James Huberty shot and killed 21 people, including children, at a McDonald's in San Ysidro, California, in July 1984. A police sharpshooter killed Huberty an hour after the rampage began.

Prison guard George Banks killed 13 people, including five of his children, in Wilkes-Barre, Pennsylvania, in September 1982. He was sentenced to death in 1993 and received a stay of execution in 2004. His death sentence was overturned in 2010.

In October 1991, George Hennard crashed his pickup through the plate-glass window of Luby's Cafeteria in Killeen, Texas, before shooting 23 people and committing suicide.

Waco Siege Feb to April 1993. Confrontation with weapons

between Branch Davidians Christian religious group and joint forces of American federal (FBI) and Texas state law enforcement and the US military. A shameful exercise in which 86 people died and the Mt Carmel Center burned to the ground. The Oklahoma City bombing was said to be a retaliatory attack later in April 1995.

Feb 1993 first World Trade Center attack by Islamic extremists Ramzi Yousef, Eyad Ismoil using a car bomb. 6 people killed, 1000+ injured.

Alfred P. Murrah Federal Building, Oklahoma City Bombing April 1995 by Timothy McVeigh and Terry Nichols as a revenge for the Waco siege. Truck bomb killing 168 and 680+ injured. Domestic terror attack against Government.

Students Eric Harris and Dylan Klebold brought guns and bombs to Columbine High School in Littleton, Colorado, in April 1999. The students gunned down 13 and wounded 23 before killing themselves.

Mark Barton walked into two Atlanta trading firms and fired shots in July 1999, leaving 9 dead and 13 wounded, police said. Hours later, police found Barton at a gas station in Acworth, Georgia, where he pulled a gun and killed himself. The day before, Barton had bludgeoned his wife and his two children in their Stockbridge, Georgia, apartment.

Sept 2001 Twin Towers of World Trade Center, Manhattan New York and the Pentagon in Arlington County, Virginia by hijacked commercial aircraft. 2,996 people killed (includes 19 terrorists) and injuries of 6,000+ by Islamic terror group al-Qaeda.

Virginia Tech student Seung-Hui Cho went on a shooting spree on the school's campus in April 2007. Cho killed two people at the West Ambler Johnston dormitory and, after chaining the doors closed, killed another 30 at Norris Hall, home to the Engineering

Science and Mechanics Department. He wounded an additional 17 people before killing himself.

Michael McLendon's 10 victims: McLendon shot and killed his mother in her Kingston, Alabama, home, before shooting his aunt, uncle, grandparents and five more people. He shot and killed himself in Samson, Alabama, in March 2009

Jiverly Wong shot and killed 13 people at the American Civic Association in Binghamton, New York, before turning the gun on himself in April 2009, police said. Four other people were injured at the Immigration Center shooting. Wong had been taking English classes at the center.

A military jury convicted Army Major Nidal Hasan of 13 counts of premeditated murder for a November 2009 shooting rampage at Fort Hood, Texas. Thirteen people died and 32 were injured.

James Holmes pleaded not guilty by reason of insanity to a July 2012 shooting at a movie theater in Aurora, Colorado. Twelve people were killed and dozens were wounded when Holmes opened fire during the midnight premiere of 'The Dark Knight Rises.' He was sentenced to 12 life terms plus thousands of years in prison.

Sandy Hook Elementary School in Newtown, Connecticut, December 2012. Adam Lanza opened fire in the school, killing 20 children and 6 adults before killing himself. Police said he also shot and killed his mother in her Newtown home earlier.

On a rooftop at the Washington Navy Yard police discover aftermath of a shooting rampage in the nation's capital in September 2013. 12 people and perpetrator Aaron Alexis were killed.

Boston Marathon Bombs April 2015 by Tsarnaev brothers. 6 deaths and 280 injured. Islamic terrorism.

Umpqua Community College- there was a deadly shooting at the school in Roseburg, Oregon, in October 2015 where 9 people were killed and at 9 were injured, police said. The gunman, Chris Harper-Mercer, committed suicide after exchanging gunfire with officers.

Emanuel African Methodist Episcopal Church in Charleston, South Carolina, June 2015. Police said Dylann Roof opened fire inside the church, killing nine people. According to police, Roof confessed and told investigators he wanted to start a race war.

In December 2015, two shooters killed 14 people and injured 21 at the Inland Regional Center in San Bernardino, California, where employees with the county Health Department were attending a holiday event. The shooters, Syed Rizwan Farook and his wife Tashfeen Malik, were later killed in a shootout. The pair was found to be radicalized extremists who had planned the shootings as a terror attack.

Orlando, Florida June 2016: An American-born man gunned down 49 people early Sunday at a gay nightclub in Orlando, the deadliest mass shooting in the United States. The gunman, Omar Mateen, 29, of Fort Pierce, Florida, had been interviewed by the FBI in 2013 and 2014 but was not found to be a threat. Mateen allegedly called 911 during the attack to pledge allegiance to ISIS. Orlando police shot and killed Mateen. Some dispute as to whether a genuine terror attack or a revenge attack specifically targeting the gay community.

Some Massacres to US Citizens Occurring Outside the US:

Jonestown was the name for the Peoples Temple Agricultural Project formed by an American religious organization under the leadership of Jim Jones, in north western Guyana. November 18, 1978, over 900 people died in the remote commune. A total of 909 Americans died in Jonestown, all but two from apparent cyanide poisoning

Lockerbie, Scotland December 1988. Pan Am flight 103 from Frankfurt to Detroit destroyed by a Libyan terrorist bomb, killing all 243 passengers and 16 crew plus killing 11 more people on the ground. Of the 270 total fatalities, 189 were American citizens and 43 were British citizens. Twenty-one other nationalities were represented.

June 1996 Khobar Towers bombing in Khobar, Saudi Arabia by Hezbollah al Hejaz. Truck bomb killing 19 American servicemen and injuring 498 of various nationalities. Iran and Hezbollah attributed to the attack. Bomb was said to be a mixture of gasoline and explosive powder placed in the tank of a sewage tanker truck equivalent to 11000 tonne TNT.

Aug 1998 United States embassy bombings where simultaneous truck bomb explosions in two East African cities killed 224 people (including 12 Americans). One was at the US Embassy in

Dar es Salaam, Tanzania, the other at the US Embassy in Nairobi, Kenya. 4000+ wounded. Carried out by Osama bin Laden's al Qaeda.

Oct 2000 USS Cole terrorist attack by al Qaeda suicide bombers Aden, Yemen. 19 killed, 39 injured. The terrorist attack against the United States Navy guided-missile destroyer USS Cole occurred while it was harbored and being refueled in the Yemeni port. A small fiberglass boat carrying explosives and two suicide bombers approached the port side of the destroyer and exploded, creating a 40-by-60-foot gash in the ship's port side

Other Titles by Tom Law:

Nuclear Islam   3rd Edition

ISBN   9780994315793

This expose on what our future holds if we continue down the nuclear road looks at the various scenarios from conventional nuclear power plants. Also discusses the causes and outcomes of Islamic terror and how we can heal the divisions between the various religions on the planet. Population expansion is beyond our control- taken together with finite resources, the planet faces some tough times ahead!

Elementum Carbone   2nd Edn.

ISBN   9780994315755

This book explores the evolution of the Earth and demonstrates how urgent we need to turn around our consumerism and traditional thought patterns if we are to counter and avert a global catastrophe in the next seventy years. Makes some suggestions but Tom admits he doesn't have all the answers. Well illustrated and not too difficult a read on a complex issue.

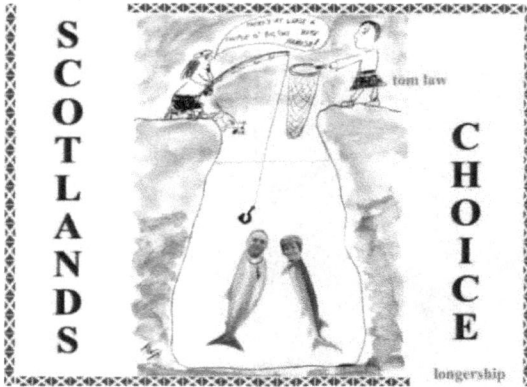

Scotlands Choice
ISBN   9781500463205

Tom Law takes a humorous look at the days leading up to the Scottish Referendum on independence in cartoon form. Not to be taken too seriously!

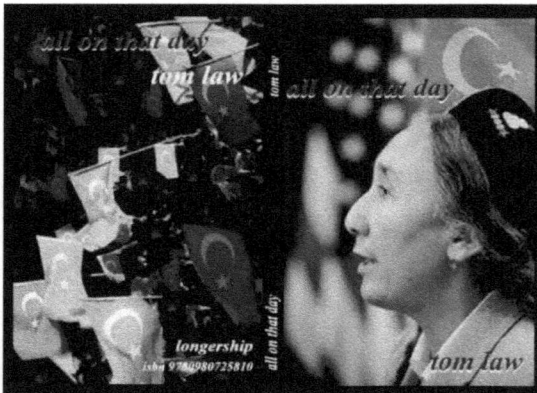

All on that Day
ISBN   9780980725810

The three horrific days in Urumqi in the far west of China when the Han Chinese with the assistance of the Army put down a demonstration by the Uighurs praying for an independent state. The politics and cruel aftermath inflicted by a giant bully on the original inhabitants of the region.

boy in blue raincoat

tom law   LONGERSHIP

Boy in Blue Raincoat
ISBN   9780980725841

Story of a young boy with an independent and robust spirit living in a timber mill town in Eastern Victoria during the 1960s. He finds both friendship and love in most unexpected ways but life's hammer awaits his next move. Admixture of youthful happiness and pathos.

Return to Animalia
ISBN   9780994315700

Politics of contemporary Australia as seen through the eyes of perhaps a very British Australian. A disquieting diatribe on many issues with solutions given as possible suggestions. Could easily be construed as unapologetic extremism by some, but sensible remedies by others depending on one's perspective!

China Collection
ISBN   9780980725889

A collection of images, poems and anecdotes on contemporary China from the author's viewpoint whilst living and working there.   The populous forge through each day juggling their real life problems and expectancies against an eternal background of totalitarianism. They must tread wearily.

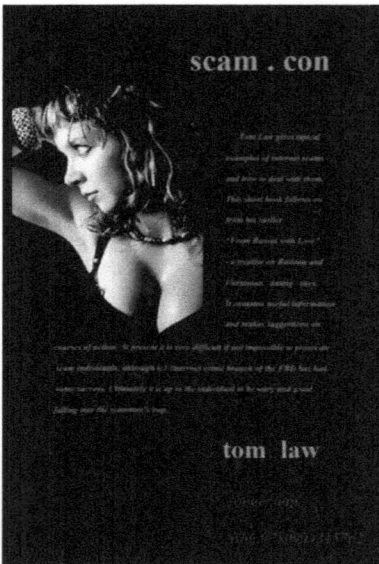

scam.con   2nd Edn.

ISBN   9780994315762

Tom Law explores the many internet scams that daily drop into our electronic mail box. He looks at some of the more humorous attempts by those wily Nigerians that try, by so many devices, to get that Western Union transfer to their greedy coffers. Provides some advice on what to look for and how to avoid an ever increasing sophistication on the art of scamming!

From Russia with Love   2nd Edn.

ISBN   9780994315748

The business of love is fraught with calamities, pitfalls and is sometimes extremely expensive. Why does the aging male seek out internet brides in the knowledge that it will most likely be a scam and will end in tears plus a depleted wallet? Tom Law looks at the reasons behind this behaviour and delves into the sometimes seedy and corrupt side of the websites that promise so much. Are there some stories of true love found and happy ever afters?

www.ingramcontent.com/pod-product-compliance
Lightning Source LLC
Chambersburg PA
CBHW022103280326
41933CB00007B/242